EARTH DAY
AND THE
ENVIRONMENTAL
MOVEMENT

STANDING UP FOR EARTH

CHRISTY PETERSON

TWENTY-FIRST CENTURY BOOKS / MINNEAPOLIS

FOR DAD AND MOM, WHO TAUGHT ME HOW TO CHANGE THE WORLD

I would like to thank Robert Tuck, Emma Peterson, and Larry Hamilton Jr. for their help on this book. I would also like to thank my family for their support. I couldn't have done it without you.

Text copyright © 2020 by Lerner Publishing Group, Inc.

Twenty-First Century Books
An imprint of Lerner Publishing Group, Inc.
241 First Avenue North
Minneapolis, MN 55401 USA

For reading levels and more information, look up this title at www.lernerbooks.com.

Main body text set in Adobe Garamond Pro.
Typeface provided by Adobe Systems.

Library of Congress Cataloging-in-Publication Data
Names: Peterson, Christy, author.
Title: Earth Day and the environmental movement : standing up for Earth / Christy Peterson.
Description: Minneapolis : Twenty-First Century Books, [2020] | Audience: Ages: 13–18. | Audience: Grades: 9–12. | Includes bibliographical references and index. |
Identifiers: LCCN 2019003593 (print) | LCCN 2019014562 (ebook) | ISBN 9781541579262 (eb pdf) | ISBN 9781541552814 (lb : alk. paper)
Subjects: LCSH: Earth Day—History—Juvenile literature. | Environmentalism—History—Juvenile literature.
Classification: LCC GE195.5 (ebook) | LCC GE195.5 .P47 2020 (print) | DDC 394.262—dc23

LC record available at https://lccn.loc.gov/2019003593

Manufactured in the United States of America
1-45657-41684-9/6/2019

CONTENTS

CHAPTER 1
ENOUGH IS ENOUGH 4

CHAPTER 2
SENATOR NELSON'S BIG IDEA 18

CHAPTER 3
TWENTY MILLION STRONG 34

CHAPTER 4
A FRAMEWORK FOR PROGRESS 45

CHAPTER 5
GONE GREEN 60

CHAPTER 6
A CHANGING CLIMATE 72

CHAPTER 7
A NEW RESOLVE 96

GLOSSARY 108

SOURCE NOTES 109

SELECTED BIBLIOGRAPHY 115

FURTHER INFORMATION 115

INDEX 117

ENOUGH IS ENOUGH

The skies over Southern California on January 28, 1969, signaled a return to typical mild winter weather. Over the weekend, a record-breaking storm brought drenching rains that scoured local streams and storm drains, washing piles of debris into the sea, but Tuesday promised just a hint of moisture. As lunchtime approached, Santa Barbara's residents went about their usual activities. But 6 miles (9.7 km) off the Pacific coast and 3,479 feet (1,060 m) under the waves, a drilling rig was about to strike disaster.

At a quarter to eleven in the morning, the crew on Union Oil's Platform A began to pull a pipe from a newly drilled oil well to change the drill bit. Suddenly, a 90-foot (27 m) geyser of mud, oil, and natural gas gushed from the pipe. Heavy drilling mud—a thick mixture of water, clay, and chemicals that workers pumped into the shaft to lubricate the drilling equipment and stabilize the well—had failed to compensate for the pressure difference between the shaft and the pocket of oil and gas the well had just penetrated. If the workers didn't address the situation quickly, the entire well could explode.

The explosion at Union Oil Platform A caused millions of gallons of oil to spill out into the Santa Barbara Channel off the coast of Santa Barbara, California.

Slogging through thick mud and oil that covered the platform, the crew worked to screw down a valve that would allow them to seal the well. But the extreme pressure—more than 1,000 pounds per square inch (70 kg per sq. cm)—doomed their efforts. An explosion was imminent. All unnecessary crew members quickly evacuated the platform.

A handful of workers remained to try to avert disaster. They dropped the drill pipe back into the well and slammed enormous steel blowout preventers on top. Thirteen minutes after the initial burst from the pipe, workers capped the well. That solved the immediate problem of oil gushing onto the platform, but pressure building below the seabed had nowhere to go. Minutes later, the shaft blew out. The force of the underground explosion forced pressurized oil and gas into the adjacent rocks. Cracks in the seafloor appeared in five places. Minutes after the blowout preventers had been locked down, oil and gas began to spew into the ocean.

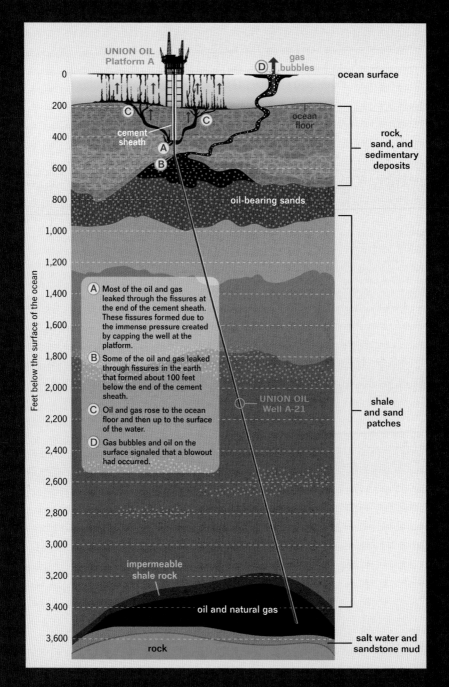

Thick, black oil and churning natural gas rose to the surface, enveloping Platform A in a bubbling cauldron. But two and a half hours after the accident, Union Oil assured the Coast Guard that everything was fine and that it didn't need help. As work continued on Platform A to stop the leaks, word went out to company officials. Meanwhile, a few miles away, thousands of Santa Barbara residents remained unaware of the accident.

WORD LEAKS OUT

On Wednesday morning, a crew aboard a Coast Guard helicopter learned the full scale of the disaster. Miles of ocean lay under a blanket of oil. The crew on the platform worked to reconnect the pipe so they could pump in more drilling mud, and crews at sea dropped detergent to break up the slick. Union Oil flew in cleanup equipment from Texas oil fields.

At the *Santa Barbara News-Press*, reporter Bob Sollen received an alarming anonymous phone call. A voice at the other end of the line said, "The ocean is boiling around Platform A." Though Sollen pressed the caller for more details, the voice simply repeated, "The ocean is boiling around Platform A. Goodbye."

By noon on January 29, Union Oil officially notified local officials of the spill. On the news, the company assured the public that there "was nothing to worry about. Everything was under control." The reality was far grimmer—upwards of five thousand barrels, or 210,000 gallons (794,936 L) a day, poured into the ocean.

Initially, calm winds kept the slick out at sea; all residents could do was watch and wait. On Wednesday, they waited. On Thursday, they waited. Finally, on Friday, January 31, when the oil slick had grown to 323 square miles (837 sq. km) and offshore winds died down, the first drops of oil reached California beaches.

Over the next days, the thick, black slick crept along miles and miles of shoreline. It engulfed offshore islands and choked off Santa

BEFORE EARTH DAY—RIVER ON FIRE

Five months after oil blanketed California's beaches, at 11:56 a.m. on Sunday morning, June 22, 1969, firefighters in Cleveland, Ohio, responded to a call. Sparks from a passing freight train had ignited the Cuyahoga River. Firefighters aboard a fireboat battled the inferno, which rose five stories above the river. Units from three battalions worked onshore to douse flames engulfing two railroad bridges.

The next day, a Cleveland newspaper ran a 181-word story on page 11-C reporting that the fire had caused $50,000 in damage to the two bridges, forcing one to close. It noted that the firefighters had brought the fire under control in twenty-four minutes. In Cleveland a river fire wasn't news—it had happened more than a dozen times before. The damage from the 1969 fire was minimal compared to previous blazes. Five people had died in a 1912 fire, and a 1952 fire had caused $1.3 million in damages.

The Cuyahoga was in trouble. A slaughterhouse dumped blood and animal parts, and mills colored the water orange with pickling acid. In its heaviest polluted areas, its waters were lifeless. Even tenacious species like leeches and sludge worms, which usually thrive on wastes, couldn't survive.

The 1952 Cuyahoga River fire destroyed three tugboats, three buildings, and shipyards along the riverbank.

Out on the blackened beaches and at rescue centers, people of all ages and backgrounds worked to help oil-soaked birds and other wildlife. Some drove from Los Angeles and other cities miles away, determined to do their part. But the army of volunteers was no match for the devastation. Frightened birds sometimes plunged farther into the muck to escape rescuers. Though some animals were pulled out alive, most later died at the cleanup centers.

Barbara Harbor. Oil-soaked debris from the previous weekend's storm washed ashore. The overwhelming smell of tar drowned out the clean, salty ocean breeze and blanketed the region. Residents of local communities could do nothing as the tide deposited choking black goo on once-pristine beaches. The slop, slop, slop of oil replaced the comforting roar of the ocean. Oil-coated seabirds struggled and died. Dead fish, seals, and whales began to wash up on the beaches. People stood on the beach, helpless, and cried.

Oil-covered seabirds washed up on shore in Santa Barbara as a result of the Platform A spill.

THE CLEANUP BEGINS

Union Oil worked nonstop to plug the leaks, while company crews and state and national officials descended on the region to coordinate the cleanup. Their efforts did little to ease the anxiety of local residents. Chemical dispersants to break up the slick and prevent it from reaching shore proved ineffective. Rough seas hampered attempts to corral and pump the oil. Local fishers, their livelihoods sidelined by the disaster, worked with the company to keep oil out of Santa Barbara Harbor. But booms deployed to corral the oil, along with other measures, worked only in calm seas—oil soon crept right up to the harbormaster's office. On miles of oil-soaked beaches, workers spread straw to soak up the thick goo washing ashore. They gathered the sullied straw and oil-soaked storm debris and carted it away to local landfills but quickly ran out of places to deposit it.

Word of the disaster landed on the front pages of newspapers from the *Los Angeles Times* to the *Washington Post.* The worst oil spill in the nation's history sparked shock and outrage. How could this happen? Why were cleanup efforts so inadequate?

On February 4 and 5, the US Congress held hearings to find out what had happened. During the hearings, Santa Barbara County supervisor George H. Clyde expressed the frustrations of local residents over the government's handling of the crisis, especially the failure of Interior Secretary

Miles of shoreline were coated with crude oil, including Hobson Beach in Santa Barbara, California, after the 1969 Union Oil leak.

The *New York Times* quote "I'm amazed at the publicity for the loss of a few birds" further damaged an already-tenuous relationship between Union Oil and residents affected by the spill. Fred Hartley insisted he never said those words. Who was right? The *New York Times* or Hartley? The newspaper did take some liberty with the quote. Hartley had said, "I am always tremendously impressed at the publicity that death of birds receives versus the loss of people in our country in this day and age." Perhaps the real question is, Did the paper misrepresent Hartley, or did the two quotes essentially mean the same thing?

Walter Hickel to take immediate, decisive action to freeze oil production in the channel. Union Oil president Fred Hartley, along with other oil and gas experts, was called to account for the events leading up to and directly after the spill.

On February 6, the *New York Times* reported that Hartley had told the Senate Subcommittee on Air and Water Pollution: "I'm amazed at the publicity for the loss of a few birds." Though the paper retracted the statement a few days later after a vehement denial from Hartley, the damage was done. Anger over the sullying of beaches, the death of wildlife, the loss of livelihoods, and the apparent indifference of company officials pushed residents into action.

"WE'VE GOT TO GET OIL OUT!"

On January 30, 1969, even before oil had reached the shore, a friend flying over Platform A called artist Bud Bottoms to tell him the extent of the damage. He finally yelled, "We've got to get oil out!"

His boss, Marvin Stuart, suggested shortening "get oil out" to GOO! And an activist group was born. Members of GOO! began to organize. They circulated a petition demanding the shutdown of offshore oil production. Students collected oil from blighted beaches in flasks and mailed them to local and national lawmakers. People displayed bumper stickers and signs. At another event, participants brought mirrors to the beach and reflected sunlight onto Platform A.

Demonstrations became a common sight in Santa Barbara. Though protests were ubiquitous in 1969, when people across the United States regularly rallied against the war in Vietnam, the crowds in Santa Barbara weren't the usual mix of students and counterculture types. The town's population of seventy thousand was largely educated and financially comfortable. Oil spill protesters were businesspeople and homemakers, socialites and local government officials, and students and clergy.

Public action extended beyond waving signs. Santa Barbara's residents lobbied Congress. Supporters in the House and Senate introduced bill after bill related to offshore oil drilling, seeking to ban or delay further drilling, buy back the oil leases that gave companies the right to drill in certain areas, and create marine sanctuaries. They also wrote letters—lots of letters—expressing their anger about the inadequacy of the cleanup and lack of state and national government action. On February 11, 1969, the *Santa Barbara News-Press* forwarded thousands of letters with the following note:

> Because the *News-Press* believes these letters are an accurate reflection of local public opinion regarding offshore oil exploration in the Santa Barbara Channel we are sending tearsheets of all of them, as well as the daily *News-Press* editorials on the subject, to President Nixon and all elected officials representing this area at the federal and state levels.

NO END IN SIGHT

As citizens organized, Union Oil continued work to stop the flow of oil in the channel. At the platform, crews started up production on neighboring wells to try to reduce pressure. They also pumped in heavy drilling mud into the cracks in the seafloor to halt the flow of oil from below. Finally, on February 8, 1969, the heavy mud seemed to have slowed the flow of oil. Following that, crews injected cement into the blown-out well. Eleven days after the accident, Union Oil reported that it had successfully sealed the leak. But an estimated 2.3 million gallons (8.7 million L) of oil had spilled into the ocean.

But the company's proclamation wasn't entirely accurate. Because the blowout had compromised the seafloor, oil continued to flow into the ocean. On February 24, less than a month after the accident, another well on Platform A blew. Oil began flowing again, and another layer of thick oil blanketed the beaches. The *Santa Barbara News-Press* added a daily feature to its paper announcing how many days the leak had continued.

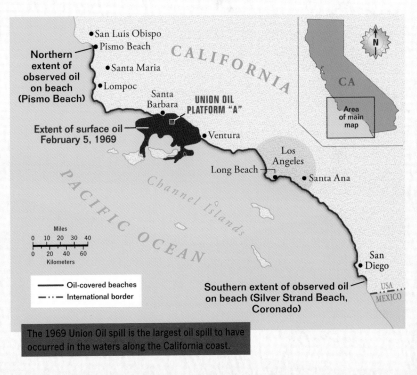

The 1969 Union Oil spill is the largest oil spill to have occurred in the waters along the California coast.

As winter slid into spring, while oil still leaked into the ocean and cleanup dragged on, the extent of the spill's damage became clearer. Commercial fishing operations brought in 250,000 pounds (113,400 kg) less than the year before between December 1968 and March 1969. Tourists avoided the area, costing local businesses about $1 million in the eight months after the spill.

But a more significant effect of the spill was the loss of public trust. Research conducted by the attorneys working on a willful misconduct lawsuit revealed that Union Oil had received a waiver related to the protective casing that oil companies were required to place around an oil well as they drilled into the seabed. The regulation required the casing to extend 880 feet (268 m), but Union Oil received permission to extend the casing only 239 feet (73 m). Had the US Geological Survey required the full casing, the disaster may not have occurred.

Nixon, Congress, and other government officials repeatedly sympathized and promised to make changes. Spurred by the letters mailed to him by the *News-Press*, Nixon visited the affected areas on March 21. Prior to the visit, bulldozers worked feverishly on Leadbetter Beach in Santa Barbara, fastidiously cleaning it of oil, seaweed, and any other debris. Nixon and his entourage arrived via helicopter.

The president stood on a clean, sanitized beach, spoke to workers dressed in fresh white coveralls who wielded small rakes, and made

"WHEN WILL IT END"

The *Santa Barbara News-Press* continued to run a daily tally of the leak throughout 1969. Ten days before Christmas, a pipeline at Platform A ruptured, spilling thousands of gallons of oil. Five days before Christmas, the caption for the daily tally read, "Oil Spill in its 327th Day. When Will It End?"

a few remarks to the public. A crowd, separated from the president by restraining cordons many yards away, yelled "Get Oil Out! Get Oil Out."

Nixon told those affected, "The Santa Barbara incident has frankly touched the conscience of the American people." But none of the drilling-related bills introduced in the days after the spill passed in Congress.

A temporary ban on offshore drilling immediately following the spill was to "'continue indefinitely' while exhaustive studies' were made." Instead, it was lifted on April 1. Meanwhile, oil continued to leak into the channel.

THE LONG BATTLE BEGINS

On Easter Sunday, a few hundred people gathered along Santa Barbara's still-beleaguered waterfront for a rally. The last speaker suggested to those gathered that they march to Stearns Wharf, a pier where oil companies stored equipment and supplies. Most of the crowd agreed and made their way downtown. They signed petitions and pledged to appeal to the city council to end the oil company's lease at the wharf.

As the crowd broke up, two trucks arrived, ferrying supplies for the oil company. The people refused to make way, and a dozen or so sat down in front of the lead truck. Police arrived, but that inspired more people to sit down. Everyday residents—businesspeople, university professors, pastors, parents, and teachers—all had had enough. The unplanned protest lasted ninety minutes, and in the end, the trucks left.

The victory was temporary. The trucks returned after the protest broke up. Still, the community had asserted itself. The battle wouldn't be over in a week, a month, or even a year. Community members were determined to protect their homes, their children, and their future by fighting oil drilling off the Southern California coast.

BEFORE EARTH DAY— MOUNTAINS OF TRASH

The production of throwaway consumer products boomed following World War II (1939–1945). Buying goods was a way to help the country recover economically. Disposable razors, TV dinners, plastic toys, paper plates, aluminum cans, fast-food packaging, and ballpoint pens—you name it, you could buy it and toss it. But eventually, cities across the country began to run out of room to put their trash.

New York City dealt with its trash just as most places in the United States did—burn it or find an out-of-the-way spot to dump it. Sometimes that dumping ground was the ocean. Most often, it was "unusable" real estate such as wetlands, marshy shorelines, hidden gulches, or any unusable land out of sight of wealthier neighborhoods.

Fresh Kills Landfill on Staten Island opened in 1948 on wetlands city planners had deemed useless for city expansion. The landfill was supposed to operate for only three years, but the city's urgent need for a place to dump 30,000 tons (27,216 t) of trash daily overwhelmed its "temporary" status. Fresh Kills grew into the world's largest landfill. Its mountain of trash dwarfed the Great Pyramid of Giza.

The Fresh Kills Landfill was in operation for fifty-three years. It closed in 2001.

People in Santa Barbara County weren't alone in their frustration over the lack of local, state, and federal action to address serious environmental problems. Activists around the country had been raising awareness for years about choking smog, polluted lakes, mountains of trash, plummeting wildlife populations, and harmful pesticides. But activist activity was fragmented. Those concerned about protecting habitat for fish and game focused efforts on that issue alone. Those concerned about smog focused on smog. Those focused on water pollution focused on water pollution and so on.

This fragmentation, along with a lack of government oversight, allowed companies to get around or outright ignore environmental laws enacted in the previous decades. Significant, long-lasting change required a unified, sustained effort from the public, the media, and lawmakers at all levels of government. The shocking environmental disaster in Santa Barbara captured the attention of the entire nation and created an opportunity for real change. The country needed a leader who would seize the moment.

CHAPTER 2

SENATOR NELSON'S BIG IDEA

I n August 1969, as cleanup, protests, and lawsuits dragged on, a water quality conference convened at the University of California, Santa Barbara. Among the speakers was Gaylord Nelson, a senator from Wisconsin. Nelson was one of the few members of Congress focused on environmental issues. The environment had been his top priority since he had first been sworn in on January 8, 1963. In his first speech on the Senate floor, he had urged support for a bill to ban phosphate detergents. The bill failed.

Nelson's legislative efforts did not fare much better. In 1966, four years after Rachel Carson's book *Silent Spring* raised the public's awareness of the dangers of DDT and other pesticides, Nelson created a bill that would ban DDT. He could not recruit a single cosponsor, and the bill died before it even came to a vote. A series of water pollution bills Nelson attempted to introduce the same year also died. Though Congress did pass legislation related to air and water pollution in the mid-1960s, efforts at the federal level were largely limited to scientific study, not regulation.

Besides Congress's limited action, the media paid little attention to environmental concerns. The Vietnam War raged overseas, and battles to ensure civil rights for all races and equal rights for women played out in the streets at home. The space race captured the imagination of the nation. Opinion polls in years leading up to 1969 showed the environment was not a top concern or even a distant second.

THIS TIME IS DIFFERENT

Nelson's 1969 speech at the University of California, Santa Barbara, was part of a series of talks he had planned across the West. Despite earlier setbacks, he continued working to bring public attention to environmental issues. After the water quality conference, Nelson toured oil-stained beaches and harbors still struggling after the January spill. With these scenes fresh in his mind, Nelson boarded the plane that would take him to his next stop.

Nelson had seen the public's attention captured by searing images of oiled birds and blackened beaches. Nelson felt that the public was ready to turn its full attention to environmental issues. He was

AN EARLY FAILURE TO FOCUS NATIONAL ATTENTION ON THE ENVIRONMENT

Nelson attempted to get President John F. Kennedy focused on the environment. He urged the president to take a conservation tour of the country to raise awareness. Kennedy agreed, and the tour set off on September 24, 1963. But during the tour, the president's remarks often strayed to other topics. The media did not report on the environmental theme, instead focusing on his tax bill and a nuclear treaty. The attempt to raise awareness about the environment proved to be a colossal flop.

Nelson used images of oil-saturated birds, such as this duck, to call attention to environmental issues.

convinced that if he could mobilize the public's concern into action, Congress would have no choice but to pass legislation to establish nationwide environmental protections.

On the plane, Nelson read an article about teach-ins at colleges and universities around the country to protest the Vietnam War. As he read, an idea began to form in Nelson's mind. "Why not have an environmental teach-in and get everyone involved?" The impact could increase if colleges across the country held events at the same time. The energy of students and the concern of citizens around the country could be combined. Perhaps then Congress would be convinced to act.

The idea could work—Nelson was certain. But the lifelong politician had no experience organizing a nationwide event. For help, he turned to Fred Dutton, who had worked for such politicians as President Kennedy and California governor Pat Brown. Within weeks, Dutton produced a detailed prospectus, or suggested plan, outlining the steps to organize and run such a huge event. He urged

Nelson to create a board of sponsors to "provide legitimacy, diversity of representation, and a national frame of reference for the project." Dutton suggested that Nelson and his staff create a committee to oversee the planning, raise funds to cover expenses, and hire a small staff to focus on the teach-in. The prospectus covered specific events and activities to be planned and marketing ideas.

Gaylord Nelson (*left*) had worked with John F. Kennedy (*right*) on Capitol Hill. Nelson enlisted Fred Dutton, who had worked with Kennedy, to assist him in organizing an environmental teach-in.

Dutton had one other piece of advice: change the name. Though he admitted he didn't like the names he'd thought of—"Last Chance Day . . . Mission: Earth Rescue . . . Nature Day . . . etc."—he felt the name had to sum up the event. "Even little matters," he wrote, "like the letter head for mailings should have a flourish appealing to the young—a little far out, fresh, elemental, somewhat irreverent."

THE FIRST TEACH-IN

The first teach-in was March 24, 1965, at the University of Michigan, Ann Arbor, to protest the Vietnam War. Students and faculty held lectures and debates, put on musical performances, and screened films. The goal was to educate participants about the war and garner support for anti-war efforts without being disruptive while including a variety of viewpoints.

With Dutton's help, Nelson's teach-in idea was off and running. Though Nelson liked many of the suggestions in the prospectus, he rejected one idea: a top-down organized event. Nelson knew that he and his staff didn't have the resources to plan and run events in communities across the nation. That didn't mean they sat by and waited for the teach-in to organize itself. For three intense months, with untiring assistance from his staff, Nelson began to put Dutton's suggestions into action.

DRUMMING UP SUPPORT

On September 20, 1969, Nelson spoke before a meeting of the Washington Environmental Council in Seattle. The council was working to ban DDT in the state and to add a conservation bill of rights to the state constitution. Nelson had come to offer his support, but he added something unexpected to his speech:

> I am convinced that the same concern the youth of this nation took in changing this nation's priorities on the war in Vietnam and on civil rights can be shown for the problems of the environment. That is why I plan to see to it that a national teach-in is held.

It was a strange place for Nelson's big announcement. No reporters from national media outlets covered the event. No one expected big news to come out of a modest conservation meeting in the Pacific Northwest. But at least two local papers carried stories about the speech the next day, and a short story went out over the AP newswire.

That one small story, along with Nelson's enthusiastic stumping, was all it took. By early October, the news had appeared in the *Milwaukee Journal* and *Time* magazine. Stories in the *New York Times* and *Newsweek* soon followed. In a time when the nation received its news from a handful of newspapers, magazines, and television

BEFORE EARTH DAY— SPECIES ON THE BRINK

The widespread use of DDT following World War II proved to be the final blow for birds of prey such as eagles and falcons, whose populations had already dwindled due to eradication efforts and habitat loss. Chemicals in DDT disrupt calcium production in birds' bodies, which leads to dangerously thin eggshells. When parents attempt to incubate, the fragile eggs are crushed under the weight of the adults. Population numbers began to drop rapidly. For example, by the mid-1960s, peregrine falcon populations had declined to about thirty-nine nesting pairs, down from several thousand prior to 1940.

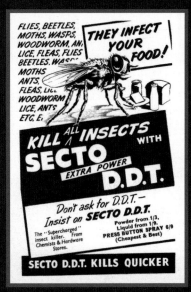

DDT was advertised as an effective pesticide through the 1950s and 1960s.

networks, this publicity was significant. The media was finally giving its attention to broader environmental issues rather than just covering disasters. Nelson's Senate office began fielding calls and opening letters from people around the country who wanted to get involved. The idea was officially off the ground, but what Nelson did next would shape Earth Day and the environmental movement forever.

AN EVENT FOR EVERYONE, BY EVERYONE

Some of the teach-in's earliest enthusiasts were college students who heard Nelson speak at a conference in October. The day after the speech, several of them made the trip to Nelson's Senate office, announcing that they were ready to run the teach-in for him. But their vision was very different than Nelson's was. They wanted a militant,

BEFORE EARTH DAY—DEADLY AIR

In November 1966, a million people lined Central Park West and Broadway to watch New York City's annual Macy's Thanksgiving Day Parade. Marching bands filled the air with festive music, and Santa Claus made his seasonal debut. The mild temperatures and calm winds were perfect for parade viewers, but the weather system responsible for these pleasant conditions also kept the air stationary over the city.

Into the still air, factories, garbage incinerators, and vehicles poured sulfur dioxide, carbon monoxide, and other harmful chemicals. City officials shut down municipal garbage incinerators and asked local energy companies to burn oil or gas instead of coal. Eighteen field inspectors were told to "forget their turkey dinners and start looking for dirty air."

By the time Thanksgiving dinner had been served and the city's residents had settled in for the night, "the pollution index had reached a high of 60.6, more than 10 points over the health danger mark," possibly the highest in New York City history.

The following morning, the commissioner of the Department of Air Pollution Control issued an alert. Apartment complexes and public buildings were asked to turn their thermostats down to 60°F (16°C). Businesses and residents were urged to limit driving. Although doctors assured the public that no ill effects had yet been observed, they advised heart and lung patients to remain indoors.

Winds finally cleared out the dirty air on Saturday. Despite earlier assurances that residents had suffered no ill effects related to the smog, a report released in December found that 10 percent of New Yorkers had suffered eye irritation, respiratory distress, or both. A report published almost a year later estimated that 168 people had died.

The polluted air hovering over New York City on Thanksgiving Day caused health concerns ranging from mild eye irritation to death.

in-your-face event, while he envisioned a peaceful, national discussion. Nelson and his staff encouraged the students to participate but declined to offer them leadership positions.

Nelson also wanted the leadership of the teach-in to be bipartisan. He worked to convince Representative Paul "Pete" McCloskey to be his cochair on the teach-in's steering committee. McCloskey, a Republican from California who supported conservation, agreed. On November 11, 1969, Nelson made a formal announcement that McCloskey would join him as cochair and that the teach-in would be on April 22, 1970.

Nelson insisted that the teach-in would be grassroots, with events organized by individual colleges and universities rather than run nationally. Nelson and his staff focused on providing information so others could plan their own events.

This approach allowed the teach-in to grow in ways that Nelson and the organizing committee did not expect. While their focus had been college and university campuses, they were flooded with letters and calls from high schools and elementary schools across the country. Some letters came from students who wanted to know how they could be involved. Others came from teachers, who wanted to plan activities for their students. Interest was so high, Nelson and the steering committee decided to hire a high school liaison.

TEACHERS GET ON BOARD

Rozanne Weissman, a National Education Association staffer, read about the teach-in and decided to try to get K–12 teachers involved. She sent several notices to every NEA state organization. By her third notice, the NEA president joined her in endorsing the teach-in. Weissman's efforts were instrumental in getting K–12 educators involved in the first Earth Day.

Nelson's staff also answered calls and letters from churches, labor unions, community leaders, and conservation groups around the country. By the end of 1969, when the offices of Environmental Teach-In had officially opened and the steering committee was fully in place, individuals, schools, and organizations around the country were already planning events for April 1970. Nelson had been correct. The people of the United States were ready to act, and the teach-in was giving them a rallying point.

A NEW YEAR

Nelson believed correctly that Congress would notice the public's concern about environmental issues if people had a national platform. In December Congress passed the National Environmental Policy Act. It created a national policy and goals concerning the environment. On January 1, 1970, Nixon signed it into law.

Against the backdrop of this success, Nelson and the steering committee began to hire staffers for the Environmental Teach-In office. Nelson invited Denis Hayes, a graduate student at Harvard, to Washington, DC, for a ten-minute interview. Hayes had traveled the world before getting his undergraduate degree from Stanford University, where he was the student body president. At Harvard, Hayes was working toward a graduate degree in law and public policy. Their conversation lasted two hours, and Nelson hired Hayes a week later as the staff director.

The rest of the staff, hired soon after, all had activist credentials. Andrew Garling, Northeast coordinator, studied civilian casualties in Vietnam and was on the Harvard Community Health Plan board of directors while still a student. Stephen Cotton, media coordinator, was an experienced civil rights worker. Bryce Hamilton, high school coordinator, volunteered with the Peace Corps and at the American Freedom from Hunger Foundation before joining the teach-in staff.

In a California courtroom in March 1969, the United Farm Workers Organizing Committee added a new grievance to its multiyear struggle for fair working conditions. For years this group had fought for farm laborers by attempting to negotiate with farmers and food processors for better working conditions and higher pay. As part of its support for striking members, the UFW set up medical clinics. As they treated farmworkers and their families, the UFW began to piece together the devastating effects that pesticides was having on its members.

To corroborate their findings, the farmworkers requested pesticide use records in Kern County. The county's agricultural commissioner, C. Seldon Morely, refused. He said that releasing this information would give away trade secrets. "Agricultural pesticides and chemicals are a way of American life today," he contended. Pesticide companies agreed, seeking an injunction—a legal action that prohibited the release of information.

In the court battle, farmworker Francisco Mendoza testified, "Every summer when I'm involved in the harvest, I get sick due to the pesticides. I get pains in my stomach, I throw up, and I get headaches. Sometimes I get chills and have itching sensations over my entire body. My eyesight has been getting steadily worse, but when I work in the field my vision gets very bad."

Labor activist Cesar Chavez (center) sought to protect farm laborers from dangerous pesticides.

"We had heard about birds and bees dying from pesticides, but we never connected it," said UFW leader Cesar Chavez to the New York Times reporter Steven Roberts. "The real problem is that the workers don't even know how dangerous this stuff is. . . . It's a subtle death, like quicksand. You don't know what's happening until it's too late."

EARTH DAY CONCERNS

Earth Day had its opponents from the very beginning. On one extreme, detractors felt Nelson's peaceful, inclusive Earth Day wouldn't go far enough. On the opposite extreme, opponents noted that April 22 was also the birthday of Russian Communist revolutionary Vladimir Lenin. They believed the choice of date belied a Communist agenda.

But African Americans and other minority communities worried that Earth Day and the budding environmental movement might draw attention away from the as-yet-unfinished work begun by the civil rights movement. Would the focus on clean air, fishable rivers, endangered animals, and other problems drown out the struggles faced by minority communities?

Cleveland, Ohio's mayor, Carl Stokes (*right*), who stood beside the sludge-filled Cuyahoga River the day after it burned and pledged to clean up pollution, shared this fear. His commitment to environmental causes was real. However, he feared that the new focus on environmental concerns of middle-class suburbanites might "be at the expense of what the priorities of this country ought to be— proper housing, adequate food and clothing."

Carl Stokes was dedicated to implementing environmental policy that addressed the needs of marginalized communities.

Nelson, the Earth Day organizing staff, and minority environmental organizers wanted to make sure this didn't happen. They believed blighted neighborhoods, smog, dirty water, lead paint, and poor housing conditions *were* environmental issues. Freddie Mae Brown, leader of the St. Louis Metropolitan Black Survival Committee, felt that dealing with environmental problems should go hand in hand with addressing economic concerns. In an interview with writer David Hendin, she said, "We have to deal not only with jobs and housing, but air and water pollution as well."She challenged the middle-class white community to make a healthy environment for all children a priority. "For the first time in our lives," she said, "there's something that can't be divided: the air."

Barbara Reid, Midwest coordinator, worked on Robert Kennedy's presidential campaign and for the Conservation Foundation. The job of western coordinator went to a New Mexico Chicano advocate, Arturo Sandoval, who helped create the United Mexican American Students group at the University of New Mexico. Sam Love, the southern coordinator, had organized both civil rights and anti-war events.

Then Nelson shifted the responsibility for the teach-in. He continued a grueling speaking schedule to encourage support for their efforts and the steering committee continued to advise the group. But coordinating and supporting teach-in events was in the hands of the Environmental Teach-In team.

FROM TEACH-IN TO EARTH DAY

On average, ten college and university groups contacted the office each day, seeking ideas and support or sometimes simply informing the staff of their plans. Thousands of teachers wanted to involve their students. Many called or wrote asking for help. The staff provided them with Hamilton's teach-in guide for teachers.

During their first days on the job, the staff made two big decisions. First, the group decided, like Dutton had mentioned in his prospectus, that "environmental teach-in" was a little too stuffy and hard to remember. They asked an advertising expert, Julian Koenig, for advice. One of his suggestions—Earth Day—seemed to fit.

The new name debuted in a full-page ad in the *New York Times* on January 18, 1970. A bold heading in huge font declared "April 22. Earth Day," followed by a passionate description of Earth Day's intent and information about the staff's efforts to help communities plan their events. The other big move the staff made in its first weeks on the job was literally to pick up and change locations. Hayes felt the office's original location near the US Capitol sent the wrong message—one of privilege and power. Instead, the group hunkered down in a dingy, ten-room office in a more modest part of town.

RACE TO THE FINISH LINE

At first, the staff hoped to directly coordinate multiple Earth Day events as well as support others' efforts, but they quickly became inundated by requests from event planners around the country. The nationwide database of events and their locations kept growing. The staff decided to limit their organizational efforts to such cities as New York and Chicago. But they influenced national efforts through a weekly newsletter, *Environmental Action*, mailed to individuals and groups in the database. The inaugural issue went out to seven thousand addresses.

Students and professors at universities and colleges around the country debated about the kinds of activities that would be the most impactful and planned events that sometimes spanned multiple days. Some opted for intellectual exercises, with respected speakers and a subdued tone. At the other end of the spectrum were ecology fairs complete with organic food, balloons, and splashy protests.

High school and elementary students and teachers worked to obtain permission for assemblies, field trips, and rallies. Students created posters and wrote poems. They invited local and national speakers to visit their schools. One school made the price of admission to their Earth Day event a squashed aluminum can.

In communities, businesspeople, homemakers, clergy, doctors, teachers, and city council members—people of all ages and backgrounds—planned events. For many, it was the first time they had been involved in this kind of organizing. They planned mini teach-ins, discussions, festivals, and parades.

As April 22 approached, plans fell into place. Early events began to occur. In February, students at San Jose State College held a weeklong Survival Faire about ecology. University of Michigan students and faculty held an Environmental Teach-In in March. Nelson continued to crisscross the country, speaking urgently about environmental issues. The Earth Day staff raced to keep up with requests for help and

FIGHTING FOR COMMUNITY HEALTH IN SOUTH LA

The third-largest oil field in the US lies in Southern California, surrounded by neighborhoods. Despite fifty-plus years of progress, the greater Los Angeles area still struggles with the worst air quality in the nation. For residents of Wilmington, just south of Los Angeles, their environmental concerns are compounded by pollution from active oil wells (*right*) and refineries.

According to the *Los Angeles Daily News*, as of February 2018, 3,468 oil wells operate in Los Angeles County. Some lie 60 to 100 feet (18 to 30 m) from homes. The residents of Wilmington, primarily Latinos and recent immigrants, are regularly exposed to unhealthy levels of benzene, hydrogen sulfide, and around three hundred other chemicals from oil extraction. These chemicals can lead to respiratory ailments and even cancer. Residents also complain of headaches, nausea, vomiting, and eye and throat irritation.

Ashley Hernandez grew up in Wilmington. Her parents saved patiently for years to buy their own home—500 feet (152 m) from an oil well. Hernandez and her neighbors routinely experienced soot-covered yards, furniture-jarring tremors, and air that burned eyes and throats. Ashley experienced severe headaches and nosebleeds.

These experiences led Hernandez to join other activists to fight for safer environmental conditions in her neighborhood. She joined Communities for a Better Environment as a teen volunteer. The group has pressed for stricter regulations on oil drilling sites and stronger oversite of site operations. In 2015 the group joined with other groups to sue the City of Los Angeles for allowing oil and gas companies to drill wells in neighborhoods without assessing the health impacts of these activities. The groups settled their suit in 2016, when the city agreed to adopt new requirements for drilling applications and to protect vulnerable communities. In 2019 California courts dismissed a countersuit brought by the petroleum industry.

Two thousand colleges, including the University of Michigan, participated in Earth Day programming.

information, as well as planning events. Their *Environmental Action* newsletter updated volunteers about impending legislation, films for Earth Day events, and information about specific issues such as lead in paint, mass transit, and environmental problems in inner cities.

When April 22 finally arrived, Nelson, the organizing staff, and the American people were about to participate in the biggest nationwide event ever undertaken.

ENVIRONMENTAL CONCERNS PRIOR TO THE FIRST EARTH DAY

AIR QUALITY

- Unhealthy levels of six pollutants—ozone, lead, carbon monoxide, nitrogen oxide, sulfur dioxide, and particulate matter—led to health issues including asthma, cancer, and premature death.

- Lead emissions from automobiles contributed to average blood levels of lead that exceeded safe levels in a majority of children.

WATER QUALITY

- Rivers around the country were dumping grounds for industrial waste, trash, and raw sewage.

- Many cities had combined sewage and storm water systems that carried raw sewage into waterways during heavy rain.

WASTE MANAGEMENT

- In the 1950s and 1960s, growing cities and suburbs began to run out of open spaces to discard their waste.

- Improperly handled industrial waste presented health risks to nearby residents when toxins made their way into soil and groundwater.

PESTICIDES AND CHEMICALS

- In January 1969 a California Department of Health survey found that 71 percent of the 774 farmworkers they examined had symptoms of pesticide poisoning.

- A 1969 survey of pesticide residue on table grapes found DDT, aldrin, parathion, and other chemicals. No one knew the level of risk these chemicals posed to consumers.

ENDANGERED SPECIES

- By the mid-twentieth century, large predators such as wolves, grizzly bears, and cougars had been virtually eliminated from the lower forty-eight states.

- The use of the pesticide DDT caused populations of birds of prey to plummet. Bald eagle numbers reached a low of 487 nesting pairs in 1963.

CHAPTER 3

TWENTY MILLION STRONG

In the continental US, Earth Day dawned first in Maine. That day, around fifty people, including students and faculty from nearby Bowdoin College, gathered around Maine state representative Barbara Coffey on the banks of the Androscoggin River. The river, which received industrial waste from nearby slaughterhouses and textile and paper mills, was among the most polluted waterways in the country—some said the worst. Local residents said that "it was a filthy open sewer. You could smell it all over Brunswick on warm days."

Coffey filled six flasks with the reeking water, which she planned to mail to the river's largest polluters and to the Environmental Improvement Commission in the state's capital. She also announced plans to take legal action if the state didn't move to clean up the river.

NEW YORK CITY

About 330 miles (531 km) south, in the nation's largest city, four hundred volunteers waited anxiously to see the result of their hard work and planning. To help participants imagine a world without cars, they obtained permission to close off a forty-five-block stretch

New Yorkers roller-skate to work to do their part to support environmentalism during the first Earth Day.

of New York's famous 5th Avenue to traffic for two hours. A five-block stretch of 14th Street would be traffic-free for most of the day. Schoolchildren wielded brooms, rakes, and shovels in Union Square all morning to prep for the afternoon's festivities.

At noon, people poured into the newly opened "park" that was 5th Avenue. The bells of Saint Thomas Church rang out over the crowd. McCandlish Phillips wrote in the *New York Times*, "There was an unearthly—or perhaps it was an earthly—quiet on the avenue. The sound of thousands of footsteps was like sand being poured on paper."

CLEARING THE AIR

A mobile air quality laboratory installed near Manhattan's Union Square recorded a massive drop in carbon monoxide in the air—13 parts per million to 2 parts per million—during the time that the two streets were closed for Earth Day events.

Employees of an architectural firm set up a picnic, complete with a quilt, tulips, and wine, in the middle of the street. Children carried signs, flew kites, and handed out flowers. People danced. The mayor strolled with his family, stopping to say a few words on the steps of the New York Public Library and onstage at Union Square.

The stage area hosted around one hundred thousand people that day. Celebrities spoke and performed, including actor Dustin Hoffman, musician Pete Seeger, and anthropologist Margaret Mead. Attendees also wandered among works of recycled art and other exhibits, along with two hundred booths decorated with balloons, banners, daisies, and violets.

The 250,000 people who participated in New York City's first Earth Day were reluctant to let the festivities end. Barbara Youngberg, who came from Queens with her two-and-one-half-year-old son, wished the celebration could be a weekly event. The *Washington Post* reported that "even the police seemed reluctant to let the fume-belching cars and busses return."

EARTH DAY IN THE BIG CITY

In Washington, DC, the halls of Congress stood mostly silent. A recess allowed members to speak at events across the nation. Outside, one thousand students marched through the streets, protesting at various government buildings. Later that evening, three thousand gathered at the Washington Monument and heard Denis Hayes deliver a fiery speech. Unlike New York City, the tone in DC was more political. In the minds of many young people who had participated in anti-Vietnam protests, women's rights marches, and the push for civil rights, the environmental movement required similar antiestablishment fervor.

Some Earth Day advocates in Boston staged a dramatic "die-in" at Logan airport. Protesters dragged six wooden coffins, with occupants, into the lobby to protest supersonic jets and noise pollution. Police arrived and ordered them to disperse. As the students began to hoist the coffins aloft and file out, police rushed in and began making thirteen arrests.

Eco-Commando Force '70 debuted in Miami in the predawn hours of Earth Day. The group of five—a marine biologist, an anthropologist, a microbiologist, a teacher, and a landscape architect—released bright yellow dye into sewage-treatment plants around the city. As the dye traveled through the system, it revealed the extent of sewer contamination in neighboring waterways. Later in the day, high school and college students joined Miami's Dead Orange Parade, a parody of the Orange Bowl Parade that followed the latter's traditional route. A grand prize was awarded for most polluted. There were twenty floats. The Statue of Liberty was on hand, complete with a gas mask. Marchers carried protest banners and walked among the floats.

> "ENVIRONMENT IS ALL OF AMERICA AND ITS PROBLEMS. IT IS RATS IN THE GHETTO. IT IS A HUNGRY CHILD IN A LAND OF AFFLUENCE. IT IS HOUSING THAT IS NOT WORTHY OF THE NAME . . ."
>
> —GAYLORD NELSON

Out west, Los Angeles, California, enjoyed a rare, smog-free day on April 22, 1970. Colleges all over Southern California held daylong events. Students from Santa Monica High School buried a car engine while sporting surgical masks. The demise of the automobile was a countrywide theme. Tommy Trojan at USC wore a gas mask, while students there also performed a ceremonial engine funeral. In Palos

Verdes, an LA suburb, sixty high school students protested the automobile not by riding bikes but by arriving at school on horseback.

Denver, Colorado, went big for its Earth Day celebration. University of Denver students created a 30-foot-wide (10 m), 17-foot-high (5 m) floating geodesic dome and paraded it five blocks down University Avenue. A student-led bicycle parade braved the cold and snow, winding through city streets on the way to the state capitol. Participants stopped to collect litter. The parade ended at the teach-in at Currigan Exhibition Hall,

Colorado cyclists demonstrate near the state capitol during the first Earth Day.

NOT EVERYONE LOVES EARTH DAY

Earth Day received broad, bipartisan support across the country, but not everyone was happy. Taxi and delivery drivers found the road closures to be a big headache. Republican candidate for Georgia governor and Comptroller General James L. Bentley spent $1,600 in taxpayer money sending anti-Earth Day telegrams warning of a Communist plot.

where colorful exhibits informed passersby about the dangers of pollution, smoking, overpopulation, and capitalism. About two dozen speakers and panelists spoke, but the highlight of the event was a speech by Gaylord Nelson who chose Denver as one of his four stops on Earth Day.

As he made his remarks, Nelson emphasized his belief that Earth Day and environmentalism should seek to benefit all:

> Earth Day can—and it must—lend a new urgency and a new support to solving the problems that still threaten to tear the fabric of this society . . . the problems of race, of war, of poverty, of modern-day institutions. . . .
>
> Environment is all of America and its problems. It is rats in the ghetto. It is a hungry child in a land of affluence. It is housing that is not worthy of the name; neighborhoods not fit to inhabit . . .

HIDDEN EARTH DAY

Coffins, car burials, crowds, and a cacophony of protests—big cities, big names, and big actions dominated the national media the evening of April 22 and the following days. CBS News with Walter Cronkite ran a special "Earth Day: A Question of Survival" that reported on events across the country. Cronkite's opening statement summed up Earth Day this way:

> By one measurement, Earth Day failed. It did not unite. Did it attract that broad cross-section of America its sponsors wanted? Not quite. Its demonstrators were predominately young, predominately white, predominantly anti-Nixon. Often its protests appeared frivolous, its protestors curiously carefree. Yet the gravity of the message of Earth Day still came through—Act or Die!

MINORITY COMMUNITIES OBSERVE EARTH DAY

One observation by Walter Cronkite in his opening words of the CBS Earth Day special was that its participants were "predominately white." He wasn't wrong—many minority communities did not participate in Earth Day, fearing that their concerns would be overlooked.

A pastor in New York City said, "While Mayor Lindsay walks the showcase streets of New York, the people of the South Bronx wallow in the same old filth and garbage. Earth Day means absolutely nothing to us—and won't mean anything until the garbage, the rats, and everything else is cleaned up."

Other minority groups chose to participate in Earth Day for exactly the same reasons—they feared that if they didn't speak up, their voices would be drowned out. While most Earth Day efforts focused on broad issues such as air and water pollution, low-income and minority activists drew attention to environmental issues unique to their neighborhoods.

Earth Day dissenters argued that places like the Bronx in New York City, which saw major declines in livable housing and quality of life in the 1950s, 1960s, and 1970s, were not receiving their share of attention.

Unhealthy living conditions in housing projects such as the Pruitt-Igoe in St. Louis were a primary concern for activists in low-income and minority communities.

United Mexican American Students in Albuquerque, New Mexico, led a street protest ending at a reeking sewage plant that had been affecting the neighborhood's quality of life. In Missouri the St. Louis Metropolitan Black Survival Committee staged a series of theatrical performances, "Black Survival: A Collage of Skits." The skits captured the environmental problems faced by the community—particularly about such environmental pollutants as lead. The performance ended with a monologue performed by a young man whose mother suffered from respiratory problems due to poor living conditions:

How long must we wait before the world is free of pollution! Must we first stand on the brink of extinction and be devoured by rats and cockroaches and wars that never end. . . . Our rich white brothers aren't concerned about poor people being unemployed, they don't care about the lousy schools. Or cops who whop the heads of the poor, and they don't care about the expressways that displaced our neighborhoods and the problems of pollution they bring in.

INTERNATIONAL INDIGENOUS YOUTH COUNCIL

In April 2016, a small group of young people set up a prayer camp on the north edge of the Standing Rock Sioux Reservation. Despite frigid temperatures, they joined together for support and in opposition to the planned Dakota Access Pipeline. Companies constructing the pipeline had broken ground three months earlier.

The pipeline's route from North Dakota's Bakken Formation oil fields to a terminal near Patoka, Illinois, crosses the Missouri River near the Standing Rock Sioux Reservation. Tribal members worry that a pipeline accident, which has happened on other pipelines around the country, could irreparably harm the river and surrounding land.

As the fight against the pipeline continued with appeals to the Army Corps of Engineers and state and national officials, the tiny camp began to grow, first by the dozen and then by the thousands. Indigenous people from nations across the United States joined in, as well as climate change activists and military veterans. The protest achieved a temporary victory in late 2016 when the Barack Obama administration ordered Energy Transfer Partners to prepare an environmental impact statement and to study alternate routes. It didn't last. The incoming Trump administration ultimately allowed the project to proceed. Oil began flowing through the pipeline in May 2017.

Demonstrators stand outside the White House on March 10, 2016, to protest the Dakota Access Pipeline.

The visible defeat—flowing oil—belies a far greater victory achieved by the youth at Standing Rock: solidarity and a brand-new organization, the International Indigenous Youth Council. Though initially made up primarily of Standing Rock participants, the International Indigenous Youth Council expanded in 2017 to include chapters across the United States. The youth council supports indigenous youth, helping them to unite and move past the repercussions of colonization that reach down through generations.

By focusing primarily on sixties-style protests, antiestablishment chants, and splashy, media-friendly stunts, the national media largely missed the breadth and depth of the day's events. Though the CBS broadcast did feature some small-town and minority efforts, it largely overlooked the actions of thousands of everyday people in small towns, schools, churches, community organizations, factories, and businesses.

But much of the life-changing, policy-changing momentum generated by the first Earth Day came from the quiet, earnest efforts of people in all corners of the country. In Ripon, Wisconsin, local businesses offered one cent per can that students collected. So 350 students picked up over twenty-five thousand cans and showed up to collect their $250.54. The story landed on the newswires that evening.

Small towns across the country showed this same enthusiasm. In Eatonville, Washington, a town of 850 in the shadow of Mount Rainier, Ms. McTee's first graders picked up trash. High schoolers made the front page of the *Eatonville Dispatch*, along with the first graders, their pickup truck filled to overflowing with trash. Six Cub Scouts from Den No. 1 in Oakes, North Dakota, picked up eight sacks of cans and trash from a 0.75-mile (1.2 km) stretch of Highway 1.

A teacher at a Council Bluffs, Iowa, elementary school brought her students to her childhood swimming hole to see the damage water pollution had done. High schoolers in Council Bluffs organized their own Earth Day observance, complete with a display of trash collected within two and a half blocks of the school, a proposal for dealing with industrial waste from chemistry students, and the screening of a student-made film highlighting local pollution issues. Smiling schoolchildren and teenagers landed on the front page of small-town newspapers across the country, along with stories of their Earth Day efforts.

Beyond the organized events reported by national news, college newspapers, or slim, small-town weeklies was an unseen phenomenon. At some level, each of the estimated twenty million people taking part

Students from the University of California, Irvine, visit a garbage dump during the first Earth Day to view the detrimental impact humans have on the environment.

in Earth Day activities made a personal decision to do something about the problems they saw around them. Joan Saxe of North Carolina picked up trash with her toddler. "I just didn't have the time to be in any organized event," she said, "so I just did it on my own and tried to raise awareness with him."

Nearly a 10th of the nation's 203.2 million people participated in Earth Day—millions of individual actions and hundreds of single-issue organizations became one movement. Earth Day became the largest public demonstration the nation has ever seen. One question remained: What would happen next?

CHAPTER 4

A FRAMEWORK FOR PROGRESS

For Dorothy Bradley, the answer to the question "What's next?" surprised her. The twenty-three-year-old had recently graduated from Colorado College with a degree in anthropology and planned to pursue a graduate degree at the University of Wisconsin. But in the lead-up to April 22, 1970, she worked to organize Earth Day activities in Bozeman, Montana, and helped create the Bozeman Environmental Task Force.

"I was suddenly feeling my sense of urgency about environmental issues and feeling my roots and sort of my calling," she said later. On Earth Day, she decided to make a run for the Montana House of Representatives. Though Harry Mitchell, a state senator, told her she was the "wrong age, the wrong sex, and the wrong party," Bradley ran anyway. She reasoned, "I'll run a campaign, and of course, I won't win. But it'd be an interesting time to voice these concerns."

"DOROTHY IS FOR THE BIRDS"

The improbability of success allowed Bradley the freedom to speak her mind and employ unusual campaign strategies. Instead of fund-raising dinners, she held a garage sale. Instead of posting the usual signs and billboards, her campaign distributed litterbags with the following slogan:

Dorothy is for the Birds
and the elk, and the
bears, and the flowers
and for MONTANA
Vote Dorothy Bradley
Montana House of Representatives

The flip side read, "It's up to you." It included a checklist for action, with such suggestions as bicycle commuting, turning off the lights, carpooling, avoiding DDT, and limiting family size. Despite that some called her a "glib, hippy kid" and "too intellectual," Bradley appealed to Montana State University staff and students, as well as the hunting and fishing community. She won her race. When sworn into office in 1971, she was the only woman out of 105 representatives and one of the youngest ever to serve.

Not all lawmakers at the time could point to Earth Day as their inspiration to enter public service. However, the enthusiasm generated during the lead-up to April 22 and the astounding success of Earth Day itself created the momentum lawmakers needed to enact legislation that would bring about significant change. And they wouldn't be starting from scratch.

A FIRM FOUNDATION: ENVIRONMENTAL LAW BEFORE 1970

Lawmakers working to craft effective environmental legislation built on a foundation of laws and regulations crafted in the decades leading up to the first Earth Day. City and state governments had tried to address environmental pollution and resource depletion as early as

OLD PROBLEMS AND EARLY EFFORTS

In the United States, concerns about environmental pollution began almost as soon as large-scale industrial operations set up shop in New England in the early nineteenth century. Cotton and wool textile mills dumped dye, bleach, and wash water. Metal works added oil contamination. Most of the factories also used waterways as sewer systems, dumping thousands of gallons of urine and feces directly into streams and rivers. Those living downstream endured the stench. The water was no longer fit for humans or livestock, and fish that people ate disappeared.

Citizens pressed for change in the courts and in state and local governing bodies. In the 1860s, New England states established fish commissions to try to reestablish fish runs decimated by water pollution and the construction of dams. In 1869 Massachusetts created a state board of health to address sewage and industrial wastes in rivers and streams. Less than a decade later, the board recommended legislation to prohibit "the discharge of human waste, refuse, and other pollutants into any water within 20 miles [32 km] of a public waterway." The law passed with generous exceptions to appease factory owners, which rendered it all but ineffective. Still, it established the state's right to weigh in on environmental issues.

In the nation's forests, fair-use laws developed during colonial times couldn't keep up with steam-powered mills and the insatiable demand for wood to power steamships and heat homes. Vermont saw 80 percent of its forests logged by the 1890s. Hillsides stripped of trees eroded into streams and rivers, inundating plant life and killing fish.

In 1894 Vermont governor Urban Woodbury said, "The owners of timber lands in our State are pursuing a ruinous policy in the method used in harvesting their timber. . . . Some measure should be adopted to lessen the wanton destruction of our forests." By 1904 a forest commission was established to oversee Vermont's woods. Reseeding began, along with calls to set aside protected forestlands.

the nineteenth century, but regulating water and air pollution locally was only partially effective. Winds blow and water flows, carrying pollution and contaminants far from their sources. For example, sewer and factory waste flowing into the Cuyahoga River eventually flows into Lake Erie, impacting residents miles from the sewers and factories responsible.

The federal government waded into the fray in 1899, when Congress passed the Rivers and Harbors Appropriation Act. Section 13 prohibited dumping any "refuse" into navigable waters except by permit. Permit-awarding was generous, so the law prevented only the most egregious, river-traffic-obstructing pollution, but it was a start.

Though momentum ebbed and flowed in the face of economic crises and world wars, over the first half of the twentieth century, efforts to address environmental degradation increased. In 1948

New legislation following Earth Day helped address the dangerous pollution that contributed to the 1969 Cuyahoga River fire.

THE BEGINNING: FIVE EARLY ENVIRONMENTAL LAWS

- **Rivers and Harbors Appropriation Act of 1899.** The act primarily concerns keeping navigable waterways clear and includes a section regulating water pollution.

- **Migratory Bird Treaty Act, 1918.** This agreement between the United States and Canada protects migrating birds.

- **Federal Water Pollution Control Act of 1948.** The act authorized federal, state, and local governments to prepare programs to address water pollution.

- **Air Pollution Control Act of 1955.** The first federal legislation dealing with air pollution provided funds for federal research.

- **Solid Waste Disposal Act of 1965.** This is the first legislation to regulate the disposal of household, municipal, commercial, and industrial wastes.

the Federal Water Pollution Control Act became the first major law to address water quality in the country. The act called for the development of programs to address water pollution and authorized the federal government to help cities and states construct water treatment facilities. Seven years later, the Air Pollution Control Act provided federal funds to research air pollution.

The air and water acts were updated several times prior to 1970, moving from research to setting standards. Work toward protecting endangered wildlife began with the Endangered Species Act in 1966, which was updated in 1969. But by fall 1969, past attempts to pass environmental legislation hadn't gone far enough and calls for more stringent legislation gained momentum.

OIL PIPELINES AND BROKEN PROMISES

The late 2010s saw a cluster of high-profile protests and legal actions in the United States and Canada aimed at halting construction of oil pipelines. American Indian nations across the country led the way. But energy companies argued—and continue to argue—that they are not building on tribal lands and therefore are not affecting tribes. They contend that accidents are rare and that adequate plans will mitigate environmental damage.

But the objection indigenous people have to oil pipeline construction is far deeper than a project's proximity to a reservation. When American Indian nations negotiated treaties with the US government, primarily in the nineteenth century, these agreements often included rights beyond land set aside for reservations. If the group had traditionally depended upon resources beyond reservation boundaries, access to these resources was often guaranteed as part of that nation's treaty rights. For example, in the Pacific Northwest, tribes not living along the Columbia River and its tributaries have the right to take salmon from the river.

Over the last two hundred years, the US government broke one treaty promise after another. When gold or other valuable resources turned up on tribal land, the government responded by redrawing reservation boundaries. And although access to resources supposedly was assured, American Indians were kept away from traditional hunting, fishing, and gathering areas.

In the mid-twentieth century, tribes began to fight for their legal rights in court. For example, in 1974 the Boldt decision in Washington State assured tribes in the Pacific Northwest a 50–50 share of harvestable salmon and steelhead in the region. It also gave them the right to manage the resource and related habitat along with state agencies.

The proposed changes to Line 3, an oil pipeline in Minnesota, threaten the same kind of treaty rights that Pacific Northwest tribes fought for in the 1970s. The route for the new line does carefully bypass reservation land. But the Ojibwe people have a legal right, granted by their treaty with the US government, to access lands and waters not part of the reservation to hunt, fish, and harvest. The Ojibwa Nation worries that the pipeline's construction and operation will impact their ability to harvest wild rice, a plant with deep cultural and spiritual significance.

For indigenous people, the fight to limit developments such as oil pipelines is not just about climate change and environmental degradation. The lands and resources are sacred to their communities, and access is part of legally binding agreements between tribes and the US government.

The Ojibwe people have harvested wild rice for hundreds of years.

THE "MAGNA CARTA" OF ENVIRONMENTAL LAW

The first legislative success attributed to Earth Day passed before April 22, 1970, and efforts to craft it began well before Earth Day. Senator Henry Jackson, a Democrat from Washington State, had worked on conservation issues in and around Florida's Everglades National Park in the late 1960s. As he looked for ways to protect the environment, he found a tangle of federal projects with conflicting goals. The Department of the Interior wanted to expand the park. New dams and canals were on the agenda for the Army Corps of Engineers, while the Department of Transportation planned a shiny, new supersonic jet airport.

Jackson believed that a comprehensive federal plan should protect the environment while prioritizing the needs of one project over another. He and others in Congress worked for years to establish environmental oversight and a national environmental policy. In 1969 Jackson created a bill that guided national environmental policy and created an advisory group that would have oversight over the federal government's environmental efforts. Representative John Dingell (D-MI) introduced a similar bill in the House.

FROM LAW TO PRACTICE

In 1946 Congress passed the Administrative Procedure Act. The act stipulates exactly how any law goes from being words on a page to actual practice. So after Congress passes a law, a designated federal agency creates regulations to achieve the intended results. Other government offices, private businesses, state and local groups, and individuals determine how they will follow these regulations. Any disputes about how to interpret the law are resolved in court.

GIVING THE ENVIRONMENT
A VOICE IN WASHINGTON, DC

As environmental advocates in local, state, and national government worked to craft legislation, other activists took on a different role—congressional lobbyists. While lobbying by special interests groups, such as auto manufacturers and the oil and gas industry, had been part of the politics for decades, prior to 1970, only two environmental lobbyists lobbied Congress. Following Earth Day, eleven more lobbyists joined the force. Five of these lobbyists were representatives from Environmental Action, a group formed by the team that Nelson had hired to organize Earth Day. In their first few months at work, they halted plans for a supersonic transport and they helped craft updates to the Clean Air Act.

Efforts on the Clean Air Act nearly failed. Two months after Earth Day, the House of Representatives rushed to pass a bill to allow polluters off the hook again if they could show that complying would hurt them economically. When the Senate began to consider the same bill, Barbara Reid from Environmental Action showed up at a meeting between lawmakers and the auto industry to request a seat in the room. She convinced the committee to meet with the Clean Air Coalition, a group advocating for tougher air quality standards, the next day. Her success made national news.

The newly strengthened environmental lobby pushed for stringent regulations and urged the public to get involved. People from across the country responded, flooding Senate offices with visits, phone calls, and letters supporting tough regulations. Their tactics worked, and the Senate passed an air pollution bill with much stronger measures than the House's version. Ultimately, the Senate's version of the Clean Air Act became law.

The environmental lobby has grown from the scrappy group of fewer than a dozen to hundreds of people and organizations advocating for Earth in local, state, and national government. These groups give individuals around the country a voice—assuring that local and national environmental concerns are considered by lawmakers as they work on legislation.

The media blitz in fall 1969 surrounding Nelson's upcoming Environmental Teach-In helped build support for legislative action. The Senate and House passed Jackson's and Dingell's bills. In December the two bills went through conference to resolve differences between the two versions. The final version became the National Environmental Policy Act, which had three major provisions:

- It created a national policy and goals concerning the environment.
- It required that all federal agencies embarking on a project consider the environmental impact of the project before beginning.
- It established the Council on Environmental Quality, which would advise the president on environmental matters.

THE BIRTH OF THE ENVIRONMENTAL PROTECTION AGENCY

Nixon signed the National Environmental Policy Act into law on January 1, 1970. The creation of a federal philosophy regarding the country's relationship with and responsibility for the environment was an important step. Federal agencies were then required to assess the potential impact of all actions, making environmental protection a priority. But no single government agency was developing regulations to meet the law's requirements, a problem that limited the effectiveness of previous environmental legislation. And because the law dealt with broad environmental themes, enforcement of related regulations would fall to many different government agencies. For example, the Department of Health, Education, and Welfare oversaw clean air laws. The Department of the Interior was in charge of water and had separate departments for air, solid waste, and drinking water. Just as

FIVE KEY ENVIRONMENTAL LAWS PASSED IN THE 1970S

- **Clean Air Act, 1970.** The Clean Air Act requires the EPA to set and enforce air quality standards and to regulate specific pollutants.

- **Federal Insecticide, Fungicide, and Rodenticide Act, 1972.** This law provides for EPA regulation of all pesticides, including distribution, sale, and use.

- **Clean Water Act, 1972.** This law gives the EPA authority to establish and enforce water pollution regulations. It also provided funds for the construction of municipal sewage treatment plants.

- **Endangered Species Act, 1973.** This law establishes a framework for protecting and restoring endangered and threatened species of plants and animals.

- **Resource Conservation and Recovery Act, 1976.** The amendment to the Solid Waste Disposal Act updated and tightened criteria for managing nonhazardous and hazardous wastes.

activism before Earth Day had been fragmented by issues, so, too, was oversight.

The president quickly charged the newly formed Council on Environmental Quality with developing regulations to carry out the law. This solved the first problem and helped begin to put the National Environmental Policy Act's ideas into practice. But it didn't address the fragmentation that had impeded adequate implementation of environmental laws for decades. In fall 1970, Nixon attempted to ease some of the confusion and streamline federal environmental oversight. He combined all or part of fifteen separate agencies dealing with everything from air and water pollution to pesticide regulation to solid waste management into one: the Environmental Protection Agency (EPA).

YOUTH CLIMATE INTERVENORS

In 2017 the Youth Climate Intervenors became the first group of high school and college students to become court-sanctioned intervenors. Intervenors are individuals or groups officially approved by the Public Utilities Commission in Minnesota to have a voice in court proceedings. They have rights not granted to the public, including submitting oral and written testimony, calling expert witnesses, and cross-examining witnesses.

The issue is Enbridge Energy's request to build 337 miles (542 km) of new pipeline through Minnesota's wetlands and wilderness. The pipeline will deliver 760,000 gallons (2.9 million L) of oil daily from Alberta, Canada's tar sands oil fields to Superior, Wisconsin.

Youth Climate Intervenors opposes the pipeline for multiple reasons. Tar sands, a sludgy mixture of rock, soil, and oil, must be strip-mined. An intense water-polluting process extracts the oil and creates petroleum coke, a toxic waste. The extraction creates "up to three times more global warming pollution than does producing the same quantity of conventional crude."

The Athabasca oil sands deposit in Alberta, Canada, is among the largest in the world.

Pipelines like the Trans-Alaska Pipeline (*in photo*) and Line 3 move crude oil from oil fields to refineries hundreds of miles away.

The oil is shipped, most often through long, snaking pipelines, to refineries hundreds of miles away. Spills, although rare, are devastating. A 2010 spill from an Enbridge pipeline released 843,000 gallons (3.2 million L) of crude into a tributary of the Kalamazoo River. Cleanup costs exceeded $1 billion. Youth Climate Intervenors includes members of American Indian nations who argue that the pipeline threatens wild rice cultivation areas.

The group worked for months researching, calling expert witnesses, and cross-examining witnesses. Sophia Manolis said that the group "wrote a 70-page legal brief on behalf of the youth perspective." Despite this, the Minnesota Public Utilities Commission approved the Enbridge project on June 28, 2018. On October 28, 2018, Manolis announced that the Youth Climate Intervenors will appeal the commission's decision. The group formally filed a lawsuit in December 2018 to prevent Line 3 from going forward. Other groups also filed suits, including the Minnesota Department of Commerce.

Meanwhile, in March 2019, Enbridge announced plans to delay construction until early 2020. In response, Youth Climate Intervenors posted the following on their Facebook page: "This is a relief to folks in Minnesota, because it gives time for our lawsuit and the other lawsuits against Line 3 to play out, hopefully stopping this pipeline altogether."

The newly formed EPA could create rules and regulations needed to implement environmental pollution laws. It could grant funds to groups working to protect the environment and human health. It could study environmental issues and work with state and private agencies to solve these problems. On December 1, the EPA offices opened at 1626 K Street NW in Washington, DC. The agency's job was to clean up America.

FIGHTING FOR THE ENVIRONMENT IN COURT

When Nixon signed the National Environmental Policy Act into law on January 1, 1970, he stated that "the 1970s must absolutely be the years when America pays its debt to the past by reclaiming the purity of its air, its waters, and our living environment. It is literally now or never."

Had Congress and Nixon realized the real power behind the act's provisions, the bill might never have passed. Media covered the sweeping, poetic language of the policy's goals and wondered who would be appointed to the Council on Environmental Quality. But the third provision of the bill—the requirement that federal agencies "provide a detailed statement by the responsible official on the environmental impact of the proposed action"—gave everyday citizens a voice. When government agencies attempted to conduct business as usual—often preparing scant information on a project's environmental impacts or skipping the requirement—environmental advocates responded with a flurry of lawsuits.

The courts responded, not by shutting the public down but by upholding its right to sue and by not allowing agencies to shirk their obligations. Though the act does not include a provision to *stop* a project if the environmental impact statement finds that damage may outweigh benefits, an agency is required to make alternative proposals. The true legacy and power of the act is that the environment must be considered during planning for every project and that the citizens must be informed of the project's impact. This transparency has given the public a way to hold federal agencies accountable.

The National Environmental Policy Act prioritized the environment nationally and subjected all federal projects to regulations. The Environmental Protection Agency provided guidance and oversight for many environmental laws. Together, they formed the foundation for environmental policy in the United States. But lawmakers were not done. As the decade progressed, Congress passed one environmental law after another—laws that still govern the nation's relationship with the environment fifty years later.

"THE 1970s MUST ABSOLUTELY BE THE YEARS WHEN AMERICA PAYS ITS DEBT TO THE PAST BY RECLAIMING THE PURITY OF ITS AIR, ITS WATERS, AND OUR LIVING ENVIRONMENT. IT IS LITERALLY NOW OR NEVER."

—PRESIDENT RICHARD NIXON, JANUARY 1, 1970

But federal laws alone did not change the country's relationship with the environment. Millions of Earth Day participants continued their own personal efforts after April 22, 1970. Some, like Dorothy Bradley, worked to change regulations at the local and state level. Others became involved in government by writing, calling, and visiting lawmakers to encourage them to pass environmental legislation. Many Earth Day participants didn't involve themselves in politics, but they advocated in other ways for the environment in their communities. Ultimately, the combined efforts of lawmakers, lobbyists, activists, and everyday people fundamentally changed attitudes and culture.

CHAPTER 5

GONE GREEN

Earth Day changed everything.

Not by itself, of course. The slow, steady work of activists in the decades preceding Earth Day prepared the way. But the impact of events leading up to April 22, as well as an estimated twenty million participants raising their voices on a single day, was incalculable. Nelson achieved his goal of convincing Congress that the nation supported environmental legislation. Earth Day inspired many of its participants to continue working for the environment beyond the event. This newly energized generation of environmental advocates continued working for change for months, years, and even decades. Their efforts resulted in profound changes to culture and practices in the United States.

Evidence of their work is found in obvious places, such as in driveways and at the trash bins. But Earth Day and the modern environmental movement have a far deeper reach than that—at every light switch and outlet, in cupboards and refrigerators. Environmentalism has changed how we shop for groceries, the buildings we work in, and even the books, music, and movies we enjoy. Not one aspect of life remains untouched.

MILES CLEANER

On February 20, in pre-Earth Day festivities, a strange procession walked through the streets of San Jose, California. Three local ministers, a group of female students wearing green shrouds, and a band led the way. Another group of students pushed a brand-new Ford Maverick through the streets. The parade ended at San Jose State College, next to an enormous backhoe and a 12-foot-deep (3.7 m) hole, the car's final burial site.

The car burial capped a weeklong Survival Faire, an ecology-focused festival in the lead-up to Earth Day celebrations. The Ford Maverick wasn't the only car to end its life in environmental events before and on Earth Day. In many participant's minds, the internal combustion engine reigned as the unofficial identity of the environment's problems. They imagined a future without it and invited others to do so. On Earth Day, bicycles were the symbolic vehicle of choice—even in snowy Denver, Colorado.

The internal combustion engine hasn't disappeared. More cars are on the road than ever. But every car on the road, except

PRIVILEGE AND PROTEST

Not everyone reveled in the car burial. For poor and minority students, the stunt represented just the kind of tone deafness they feared would come from the environmental movement's newfound energy. While white students focused on grand gestures protesting big-picture issues, poor and minority students struggled every day with on-the-ground environmental issues such as substandard housing and exposure to harmful pollutants. They argued that spending $2,500 on a brand-new vehicle and then burying it, when so many people had genuine needs, was inappropriate. When the two groups faced off over the car and its burial site, the assembled students took a vote—the majority voted to bury the car.

the most venerable vintage models, has been altered because of the environmental movement. In the months after Earth Day, lobbyists and everyday people mobilized to fight the weak, hastily passed House version of an air pollution bill. Their efforts succeeded, and the Clean Air Act in 1970 authorized the motor vehicle emissions regulation. It required auto manufacturers to reduce nitrogen oxide, hydrocarbons, and carbon monoxide from emissions by 90 percent by 1975, and it called for a phase out of leaded gasoline.

The auto industry pushed back, hard—sometimes because they feared what the bill would do to their profits and sometimes because they couldn't implement new technology fast enough. Fuel companies protested as well. Between the two, delays in implementation lasted years. But the standards in the bill led to advances in technology, both in the manufacturing of automobiles and in the refining of gasoline, which reduced emissions and increased miles per gallon. Every vehicle

AFTER EARTH DAY—SKIES CLEAR OVER NEW YORK CITY

New York City's air quality has improved since that choking Thanksgiving 1966. But the city still struggles with pollution levels higher than surrounding areas, and residents living in poorer neighborhoods have a higher risk of asthma and other pollution-related health issues than people in more affluent areas have.

New York City has ambitious goals to meet these challenges. The city's OneNYC plan aims to have the cleanest air of any city in the world by 2030 and to reduce greenhouse gas emissions by 80 percent by 2050. In observance of Earth Day 2018, the mayor's office issued a press release that included the following, "Since the dawn of the industrial revolution, New Yorkers have not been able to breathe air this clean," said Mayor Bill de Blasio. "We are making significant strides in reducing air pollution to help protect the health of everyone in our city."

on the road, whether it's a Prius or a Hummer, represents efforts to save the planet.

REDUCE, REUSE, RECYCLE: CHANGING OUR RELATIONSHIP WITH TRASH

Drive through most neighborhoods on trash day, and another Earth Day legacy becomes obvious. Bins, buckets, and cans reserved exclusively for recyclables dot the sidewalks. Some areas offer yard debris pickup as well. These services keep tons of material out of local landfills and incinerators.

Recycling was common prior to the 1940s. If an item could be reused, it was. If it couldn't, it might be turned over to the rag dealer or someone else in the community who collected and repurposed reusable material as a business. During World War II, Americans collected scrap metal, rags, bones, and even cooking fat to support the war effort. After World War II, purchasing goods was a patriotic way to restart the country's economy. This approach worked for a while, but eventually consumers had one of every gadget and gizmo. Sales began to level off. To boost profits, companies responded by increasing production of throwaway products, especially beverage containers, which up until the 1960s had been largely refillable.

An ad for the Philadelphia Salvage Committee encouraged scrap drives to aid the war effort.

By April 22, 1970, the flaws of this throwaway society had become obvious. Public service announcements urging individuals not to litter

THE ENVIRONMENT GETS A MASCOT

On September 15, 1971, iconic forest fire fighter Smokey Bear got a new buddy—Woodsy Owl. Woodsy was created by Harold Bell, a self-taught cartoonist, and others for the US Forest Service. The press release generated for his debut laid out his mission—"Work as a constant reminder to children and adults of positive ways in which pollution can be fought."

Along with his slogan, Woodsy had his own song. Television ads featured both of them throughout the 1970s and 1980s. Woodsy posters, decals, bumper stickers, and coloring sheets were distributed widely. Woodsy Owl plush toys appeared on the market along with hats and T-shirts. In the years after his introduction, 90 percent of households with children recognized Woodsy Owl. Fifty years later, a fit, updated Woodsy continues his mission, exhorting the nation to "Lend a Hand, Care for the Land."

popped up everywhere. When Earth Day arrived, picking up trash was an easy way to contribute. Across the country, post-Earth Day newspapers featured photos of smiling students with arms, bags, and vehicles full of garbage.

Of course, a single day of trash collection wouldn't solve the problem, but Earth Day provided momentum. States passed anti-littering statutes with stiff fines. Though these efforts couldn't eliminate litter in public spaces, they did make tossing trash out the car window or leaving behind picnic leftovers less culturally acceptable.

Efforts to encourage recycling got a boost from Earth Day. In the first eighteen months following April 22, 1970, around fifty ecology centers popped up around the country. These local, nonprofit organizations provided environmental education and were drop-off sites for recyclable materials. Young twenty-somethings founded most of them. Many of them had been Earth Day organizers in their communities. As interest grew, civic groups such as the Boy Scouts and League of Women Voters also began to sponsor recycling programs.

The number of drop-off points across the nation pushed into the thousands. University City, Missouri, launched a curbside newspaper recycling program in 1974, the first of its kind in the country.

The biggest leap in recycling—the outcome of the environmental movement that many Americans come into contact with daily—is curbside recycling. Woodbury, New Jersey, led the way in 1980, becoming the first city in the country to implement a mandated recycling program. Though protesters in Woodbury, New Jersey, threw trash on Mayor Don Sanderson's lawn to express their displeasure, the program reached 85 percent compliance in three months. By the late 2010s, curbside recycling programs serve almost 75 percent of Americans.

Pressure from individuals and groups has also convinced many companies to use recycled materials in their products and packaging. Recycled material is now used to manufacture items like shopping bags, food containers, and printer paper.

AFTER EARTH DAY— FROM LANDFILL TO PARK

The last barge of trash entered Staten Island's Fresh Kills Landfill in 2001. Fresh Kills entered the next phase of its existence—a transformation from the world's largest landfill into the largest new park in New York City in over one hundred years. When fully completed in 2036, it will be 2,200 acres (890 ha), or three times larger than Central Park.

Transforming a landfill into a park is not just a matter of dumping dirt on top and planting grass. An impermeable plastic liner to prevent leachate by-products—contaminated liquids—from seeping out surrounds the landfill, top to bottom. Decaying waste also generates gases such as methane and carbon dioxide. At Freshkills Park, these gases are collected in underground wells and converted to gas to heat and power homes.

NOT IN MY NEIGHBORHOOD

In 1968 residents of New York City's West Harlem neighborhood learned that a new sewage treatment plant was slated for construction between West 137th and 145th Streets. The neighborhood strongly objected to the plan, but efforts to halt the project failed and construction began in 1972.

The story of the North River plant had begun thirty years earlier when existing facilities began to overload. Originally, the Department of Public Works selected a location on the city's Upper West Side, but the city and the neighborhood protested because it interfered with development plans for the affluent area. Without consulting West Harlem residents or environmental experts, the city selected the alternate site in 1955. They did not contact community leaders until the planning was complete. In 1964 the neighborhood's planning board agreed to construction after the city emphatically assured board members that the plant would pose no hazards.

The North River plant was constructed in West Harlem against the wishes of the neighborhood's residents in the early 1970s.

The assurances proved false. When the plant finally opened in 1986, odors and health issues began immediately and worsened as the plant moved to full capacity. Deaths due to respiratory illnesses rose, and some families temporarily moved their children out of the neighborhood. When the community insisted that the city and state address air quality issues, they were mocked as "a bunch of screaming Mimis."

Over time, the work of neighborhood activists led to reduced odors and a rooftop community park on the facility, but the problems have not disappeared entirely. And West Harlem is not alone—studies have shown that pollution-producing facilities such as sewage treatment plants, landfills, toxic waste facilities, and factories are more likely to be in or near communities of color. These neighborhoods often lack the political connections and financial resources to fight back and have suffered disproportionate health and economic setbacks as a result.

"TURN OFF THE DAMN LIGHTS!"

Recycling bins and cars that emit fewer pollutants have obvious links to the environmental movement energized by Earth Day. But the impact of the modern environmental movement runs deeper than that. Every flip of a light switch, plug in an outlet, and On button pressed requires less energy than in the past.

Energy consumption was a big concern in the 1970s. Demands for oil and coal to power vehicles and electricity plants rose as the population increased and as people invested in more energy-hogging consumer appliances. Popular environmental activists warned of a time when Earth could no longer support the energy demands of the world's population. Environmental guidebooks that flooded the publishing market after Earth Day devoted many pages to reducing energy demands.

Efforts to encourage energy conservation gained urgency three years after the first Earth Day, when world events sparked the energy crisis of 1973. In October the Organization of Arab Petroleum Exporting Countries, which controlled a large percentage of the world's oil reserves, enacted an embargo on nations that had supported Israel during the Yom Kippur War, a conflict between Israel and its neighbors over territory. Oil prices jumped 350 percent. Sorry, No Gas signs became more common than Open signs. When gas stations did have a supply, customers were often limited to 10 gallons (38 L) per fill-up. Maximum speed limits were lowered to 55 miles (89 km) per hour. Since 12 percent of electricity in the United States was oil-generated, this embargo affected everyday life in numerous other ways. Stickers appeared on light switches: "Please turn off lights. Conserve energy. Save electricity." Other messages were more blunt—"Turn off the damn lights!"

The popular push for energy conservation was motivated as much by economic concerns as environmental ones, but for a time, the two goals merged. Ecology centers and environmental education resources provided tips for reducing household energy use. In a Gallup poll in the late 1970s, 85 percent of Americans reported that they were doing something to save energy. President Jimmy Carter donned a sweater, turned down the heat in the White House, and installed solar panels on the roof.

Though the country eventually moved beyond the energy crises of the 1970s, the push for energy conservation continued. These efforts include a program that kicked off in 1992—Energy Star. This voluntary effort established standards for energy efficiency for products, homes, commercial buildings, and manufacturing plants. Since 1992 more than six billion products, from light bulbs to washing machines and office buildings to manufactured homes, have earned the Energy Star label. Nearly every time a plug meets an outlet, the device being powered uses less energy than it would have fifty years ago.

GONE GREEN

Going green—a term that has come to mean "environmentally friendly or conscious"—goes deeper in American culture than recycling and energy efficiency. Walk down the aisles of any store, and see evidence of a cultural shift. The labels of tuna cans bear dolphin-safe logos. A chip bag tells how the company offsets its carbon emissions. Labels say Natural, Organic, and BPA Free.

How a fish is caught, where a company sources its power, and the presence or absence of certain chemicals in packaging are all environmental issues—and these issues matter to people. So much so that companies advertise their environmental achievements on product packaging. Sometimes these efforts reflect an environmentally friendly corporate culture. Sometimes they are merely "greenwashing," or making a product appear environmentally friendly even when the practices of the company are not.

Regardless of the real motivation, companies say that their products are safe or green because slowly, over these fifty years, consumers demanded it. For example, companies such as McDonald's have shifted away from polystyrene, or Styrofoam, packaging in response to customer concerns. Xerox and other paper manufacturers

STUDENTS SAVING SALMON

For millennia, salmon have returned to rivers and streams in the Pacific Northwest to spawn, or lay their eggs, after spending years feeding in the Pacific Ocean. But human-created barriers such as dams and culverts have reduced salmon populations across the region from millions to a few thousand.

Students Saving Salmon, a club at Edmonds-Woodway High School in Edmonds, Washington, works to reverse those losses. The club's members canvass the neighborhoods around the Shell Creek, sharing species identification with residents and asking them to note the kinds of salmon they observe and when the salmon arrive. This legwork allows the team to determine when and how many migrating salmon arrive each year and how far up the creek they are able to swim. The biggest barrier to salmon migration on the creek is a 5-foot-high (1.5 m), human-constructed waterfall. The group hopes eventually to get grant money for altering the waterway to allow salmon to move farther upstream.

Meanwhile, Students Saving Salmon works to make the accessible areas of the creek as salmon-friendly as possible. They provide information to residents about planting native plants along the stream to shade the water. They volunteer at a local hatchery, and in the spring, they release tiny coho fry into the creek. Students Saving Salmon also monitors water chemistry throughout the year to determine the creek's suitability as salmon habitat.

Coho salmon turn red and return to the exact river of their birth—in this case, the White River in Washington State—to spawn.

have increased the recycled content in their products. Over the past five decades, product changes to meet demands for more environmentally friendly options have touched almost every product we buy.

The shift in our attitudes toward the environment doesn't just show up on store shelves. Environmental concerns have popped up in music, books, and movies. Back in 1970, at the country's most celebrated Earth Day bash in New York City, celebrities took the stage to fire up the crowd and publicize the cause. A year later, radio listeners could hear Joni Mitchell belting out "Big Yellow Taxi," which bemoaned the loss of forests to urban sprawl. *The Lorax*, by Dr. Seuss, brought a message of environmental impact to children around the world. And in 1973, the movie *Soylent Green* painted a shocking picture of the results of overpopulation and unchecked pollution.

Concern for the environment continues to pervade all aspects of entertainment. Pixar's film *Wall-E* debuted in 2008 with a chilling look at a future Earth literally "trashed" by humanity. *Avengers: Infinity War* (2018) features a character who will stop at nothing to prevent overconsumption. Musicians from all genres incorporate environmental themes in their music, from pop icon Michael Jackson's "Earth Song" to country musician Brad Paisley's "Gone Green." The idea of humanity's negative impact on Earth even pops up in popular book series, such as Percy Jackson and the Olympians, where the character Grover is committed to restoring the balance between humans and nature.

From April 22, 1970, to the present day, efforts to clean up the environment and lessen our impact on the planet touch every aspect of life. Thanks to the work of politicians, activists, and everyday people, many of the green parts of our daily lives go unnoticed. Unlike Earth Day, they aren't carefully planned, special activities. Even when we aren't thinking about it, we participate in earth-friendly practices when we ride a bike or walk, take out the recycling, purchase energy-efficient appliances, flip off a light switch, or do a thousand other activities in an ordinary day.

AFTER EARTH DAY—
PEREGRINE FALCONS RECOVER

By the time the peregrine falcon landed on the endangered species list in the early 1970s, it had disappeared from the Midwest and the eastern United States. Populations in the West had declined 90 percent. The US banned DDT, the pesticide responsible for the plummeting populations, in 1972. However, it still lurked in the food web long after the ban.

State and federal fish and wildlife agencies, private conservation groups, and concerned individuals worked tirelessly to bring the birds back. A program of captive breeding boosted numbers. These birds were released into the wild to repopulate suitable habitat.

Peregrines are cliff dwellers, building their nests on precarious ledges high in the air and screaming out of nowhere to snag their favorite prey in the air. These habitat requirements led to these birds settling in unlikely new homes—skyscrapers in the nation's biggest cities. The buildings provided suitable nesting sites, and city-dwelling flocks of pigeons meant ample food supplies. By the late 2010s, an estimated two thousand to three thousand breeding pairs of peregrines lived in North America, up from just thirty-nine in the early 1970s. The birds were removed from the endangered species list in 1999.

Peregrine falcons have made a comeback since the banning of DDT in 1972.

CHAPTER 6

A CHANGING CLIMATE

The impact of the environmental movement, energized by Earth Day, cannot be understated. People from various backgrounds engage in environmentally friendly practices as part of their daily lives. But the label "environmentalist" has become fraught. On the first Earth Day, people with a variety of viewpoints and political leanings embraced the phrase. But between 1970 and 2020, personal and political positions became increasingly polarized. Efforts to address environmental concerns nationally slowed or stalled. Some began to unravel. As the divide deepened, it complicated the response to an environmental issue that both encompasses and eclipses all others—climate change.

CORPORATE PUSHBACK

Of course, not everyone supported Earth Day or the environmental movement, even in 1970. Many companies resented being characterized as the "bad guy." Robert W. Cairns, vice president of Hercules, a chemical and munitions manufacturer responsible for improper chemical disposal at several of its locations, wrote to Nelson declining his request for a donation to Earth Day efforts,

"The public is so used to using the environment as a sink for its unused and unwanted by-products, that it is hard to get them to realize the true picture or to accept the ultimate responsibility which must rest with the people."

Companies also protested that they were already doing all that could be done to combat pollution and that further regulation was unnecessary. An official at Libby, McNeill & Libby, a canned goods company, wrote, "Libby's is continuing to do everything in its power to protect the environment."

Reynolds Metals, another corporation responsible for widespread environmental damage at sites across the country, wrote, "The entire aluminum industry contributes less than a fraction of one percent of the nation's air pollution and its contribution to water pollution is infinitesimally small."

But despite the assertions, everyday Americans and their representatives in government realized that companies would not take significant action unless strong legislation forced them to do so. When it became clear that environmental legislation was forthcoming, companies responded by launching intense lobby efforts to lessen the impact. Though swift action by the environmental lobby in 1970 undermined corporate efforts to weaken statutes of the Clean Air Act, companies continued attempts to subvert and slow legislation and compliance. Because the environmental movement enjoyed broad popular and political support through the 1970s, companies' attempts to prevent furtherregulations largely failed.

THE SAGEBRUSH REBELLION

Corporations weren't the only entities fighting attempts to clean up the environment. As efforts to pass and implement stricter regulations continued in the years following Earth Day, widespread public support for government intervention began to fracture.

Efforts to clean up the Cuyahoga River began after the fire of 1969. In recent years, it received the designation "Area of Concern" under the US–Canada Great Lakes Water Quality Agreement. A formal action plan was develop for the river that identified Beneficial Use Impairments—issues that prevent the river's ability to support life and other beneficial uses—and a plan to remove these impairments. In 2017 two of the ten impairments—aesthetics and public access—were removed from the list.

But what is more profound is that life has returned to the river. Where once even the hardiest sludge dwellers died, forty species of fish reside. Bald eagles, absent from Cuyahoga County for seventy years, nest along the river. Motorboats, kayaks, and paddleboards ply the waters.

The river still faces challenges. Fish in the river are often too contaminated to eat and suffer high incidents of tumors and other deformities. River sediments still contain high levels of contaminants. Beaches often close due to high levels of fecal coliform and other bacteria harmful to human and animal health. The river still needs a helping hand, but perhaps the most telling indication of improvement is this: toss a spark in the river today, and the waters will extinguish it.

In the years since Earth Day, conditions on the Cuyahoga River have improved significantly. But there is still a long way to go.

Constituents in urban and suburban areas still largely supported legislative and enforcement efforts, but in rural areas, trouble was brewing. For many ranchers and miners in the West, the event that pushed them into action was passage of the Federal Land Policy and Management Act of 1976. This law, along with the Wilderness Act and the Endangered Species Act, changed the federal government's management practices on public lands. Previously, efforts focused on transferring federal lands to private ownership and managing grazing rights. The law repealed all previous homesteading laws, created to distribute land to the public, and directed the federal government to keep its landholdings. It also directed the government to manage the land more intensively. This new level of government involvement meant balancing the needs of multiple land users, including ranchers, miners, recreational users, and fish and wildlife.

For western cattle ranchers running cattle on Bureau of Land Management lands, the Federal Land Policy and Management Act fanned smoldering embers of frustration. Before 1976 many ranchers were already disgruntled about grazing restrictions enacted to fix damaged, overused rangeland. After the act, miners and ranchers found they had to compete with recreational users, wildlife conservation efforts, energy development, and other public demands on the land. The government also began evaluating lands used for mining and ranching for their wilderness status, which would further restrict these activities.

The policy shift meant that federal oversight would be much more intense. The ability of ranching and mining communities to use the land as they wished with minimal interference from outsiders disappeared. Residents of rural western towns saw the act as a threat to their way of life. Many felt the act swept away the last vestiges of their Wild West heritage, and they were not going down without a fight.

In July 1979, a county road crew in Grand County, Utah, rammed a bulldozer through a Bureau of Land Management roadblock and drove into lands being evaluated for a wilderness status. A local miner carved 500-plus yards (457 m) of new road into the untouched canyon floor. Protesters repeatedly destroyed subsequent barriers and ignored legal action taken by the bureau to stop them.

Mining companies punched illegal roads into untouched areas in a mad scramble to identify new mining claims before the government could inventory and set aside wilderness areas. A San Juan County commissioner stormed into a bureau office and announced, "I'm getting to the point where I'll blow up bridges, ruins, and vehicles. We're going to start a revolution. We're going to get back our lands. We're going to sabotage your vehicles. . . . You had better start going out in twos and threes, because we're going to take care of you BLMers." Soon after, vandals destroyed an entire thousand-year-old pictograph panel. Bureau of Land Management employees and their families endured bomb threats, harassment, and death threats.

As the war over who owned the public lands heated up, the Sagebrush Rebellion's bullying tactics earned a victory in the first battle. About 60 percent of lands under consideration for wilderness protection because of their archeological, scenic, or wildlife value were dropped from the roadless list.

But the real battle had just begun. Farming, logging, and mining towns across the country wished to go about their business as they always had. As the government implemented policies aimed to reduce pollution, protect endangered species, and accommodate multiple uses of public lands, rural areas often felt that policymakers in Washington, DC, ignored their concerns and failed to respect their ways of life.

A NEW KIND OF TROUBLE

With corporate pushback, delay tactics, and outright hostilities in ranching, mining, and logging towns, scientists and policymakers began to grapple with an emerging environmental crisis—climate change.

President Lyndon B. Johnson signed the Wilderness Act into law in 1964. It established a system to set aside land for preservation in as natural a state as possible. The law restricts human activities, such as roadbuilding, ranching, and mining, in these areas. At the time, fifty-four wilderness areas were created protecting about 9.1 million acres (3.7 million ha). Land has been added almost every year since the law went into effect. Today about 110 million acres (45 million ha) of designated wilderness area are set aside in the United States.

The concept was not new. As far back as 1896, scientist Svante Arrhenius speculated that burning fossil fuels could raise temperatures worldwide. In the 1950s, scientists at oil giant Jersey Standard (later called ExxonMobil) recognize that burning fossil fuels was leading to increased atmospheric carbon dioxide (CO_2). By the mid-1960s, industry-sponsored studies had already suggested that increased CO_2 levels due to fossil fuel combustion would lead to climate changes by the year 2000. Independent scientists were learning the same thing. One researcher, Charles David Keeling, patiently measured and charted atmospheric CO_2 levels for years on the top of Hawaii's Mauna Loa. His graph, known as the Keeling curve, showed an unprecedented rise in atmospheric carbon dioxide.

In 1979 JASON, a group of scientists who advise the US government on defense-related science and technology, produced a report on rising carbon dioxide in the atmosphere that concluded that "the potential problems posed by a warming climate appear sufficiently serious to justify a comprehensive research effort designed to reduce the uncertainties discussed above." The group forwarded the report to dozens of scientists, which prompted briefings to the EPA, the Council on Environmental Quality, other government agencies, and even the *New York Times*.

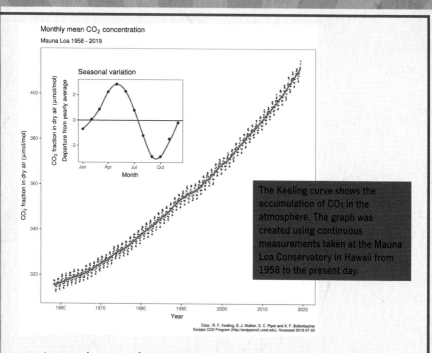

Monthly mean CO$_2$ concentration
Mauna Loa 1958 - 2019

Seasonal variation

The Keeling curve shows the accumulation of CO$_2$ in the atmosphere. The graph was created using continuous measurements taken at the Mauna Loa Conservatory in Hawaii from 1958 to the present day.

Data : R. F. Keeling, S. J. Walker, S. C. Piper and A. F. Bollenbacher
Scripps CO2 Program (http://scrippsco2.ucsd.edu). Accessed 2019-07-20

A second group of scientists assembled by Jule Charney, the father of modern meteorology, defined more clearly the problem of CO$_2$ emissions and the potential results. Their findings, in the Charney report, concluded that if the CO$_2$ concentration in the atmosphere doubles, "changes in global temperature of the order of 3 degrees C [5.4°F] will occur and that these will be accompanied by significant changes in regional climatic patterns." The report also concludes that "a doubling of atmospheric carbon will occur by about 2030 if the use of fossil fuels continues to grow at a rate of about 4 percent per year."

The Charney report provided a formal, scientific consensus about the seriousness of the problem. Growing concern among politicians and policymakers in both parties prompted the National Commission on Air Quality to convene a meeting in October 1980. Politicians, government agency representatives, scientists, industry representatives, and consultants all convened near Saint Petersburg, Florida, to come up with suggested legislative and policy solutions. The fundamental problem quickly became clear. Halting climate change and its devastating consequences would require a fundamental shift in the world's energy economy from fossil fuels to renewable resources. Consensus on practical solutions eluded the group, and its members returned to the commission empty-handed. Four days later, a new president arrived in the White House, and undoing environmental regulations was at the top of his list.

"COUNT ME IN AS A REBEL"

Ronald Reagan came to the White House riding a wave of frustration about, among other issues, increasing government regulations. His antigovernment, down-with-regulations views were especially popular with corporations and in farming, ranching, mining, and logging communities. Reagan's emphasis on economic recovery also offered hope to a country struggling through a deep slump. He won a resounding victory in the 1980 presidential election, capturing 50.7 percent of the votes to Carter's 41 percent.

In his inaugural speech, Reagan declared, "In this present crisis, government is not the solution to our problem; government is the problem." He and his administration set about to enact regulatory reform, with an emphasis on cost-benefit analysis. So for a regulation to be retained, its economic benefits had to exceed the costs of implementation and potential loss of revenue.

Reagan and his administration sought to roll back many federally mandated environmental regulations.

The administration also sought to shift responsibility for environmental protection back to the states.

Reagan's efforts to decrease regulations significantly impacted agencies working to address the climate crisis. There was talk of eliminating the Department of Energy, one of the primary agencies moving climate research forward. The Reagan administration rolled back regulations on coal mining and began to open public lands to mining and drilling. The Council on Environmental Quality found itself in danger of elimination as well. Tax breaks for and investment in alternative energy plummeted.

The administration's anti-regulation fever hit the Environmental Protection Agency especially hard. The agency lost almost 40 percent of its funding in the first year of the Reagan presidency. By 1983, 2,246 people had lost their jobs. The administration did everything within its power to roll back or weaken regulations. Sometimes agencies just failed to enforce regulations altogether.

Reagan's plans to undermine environmental protections with legislation did not fare as well. Lawmakers from both parties largely supported environmental legislation and did not go along with repealing gains made the previous decade. For example, Reagan tried to undermine efforts to phase out leaded gas. His attempts failed due to public protest and lack of congressional support.

Amid the political and agency upheaval, climate scientists continued their work. In August 1981, a NASA study found Earth had warmed already and probably would warm faster than expected.

REAGAN REMOVES WHITE HOUSE SOLAR PANELS

In 1986 Reagan removed solar panels installed by the Carter administration to provide hot water to the White House. The panels had supplied hot water for the laundry room and the cafeteria, among other areas.

In a congressional hearing March 25, 1982, Republicans and scientists agreed that the time for talk was over. Robert Walker (R-PA) stated, "We have been told and told and told that there is a problem with the increasing carbon dioxide in the atmosphere. We all accept that fact, and we realize that the potential consequences are certainly major in their impact on mankind. Now is the time. The research is clear. It is up to us now to summon the political will." Momentum was building, but would the administration play along?

The Reagan administration's answer was we're waiting for the report. In 1983 a study commissioned by Carter in 1979 finally released its findings. The report added nothing new to the science and made the same dire predictions as previous efforts. But in interviews following the release, the chair of the committee, William Nierenberg, bafflingly contradicted his own written statements, urging caution and downplaying the need for immediate action. The administration had its answer—do nothing.

THE MONTREAL PROTOCOL

Scientists and activists who had spent years attempting to address climate change refused to be defeated. To build momentum, they turned to a smaller, more manageable climate issue—ozone depletion. Ozone, a molecule made of three oxygen atoms, absorbs radiation from the sun, preventing some of it from reaching Earth's surface. This protects life on the planet from the harmful effects of too much radiation, particularly from ultraviolet B rays. In the 1970s, scientific research emerged that implicated chlorofluorocarbons found in aerosol sprays in the destruction of Earth's ozone layer. Years of activism and several studies confirmed the science. The US finally banned chlorofluorocarbons in 1977. However, a ban in the US couldn't protect the rest of the planet.

Although Reagan often used his favorite tool—cost-benefit analysis—to oppose many environmental regulations, the same approach spurred him to take action about ozone depletion. The cost to care for increased numbers of skin cancer patients was higher than taking the necessary environmental action, which prompted Reagan and Canadian prime minister Brian Mulroney to lead the way on the Montreal Protocol. The protocol was a tool for the worldwide crackdown on chlorofluorocarbons. Reagan felt this was insurance against potentially dire consequences and higher costs.

A CLIMATE SUCCESS STORY

Chlorofluorocarbons hang around in the atmosphere long after they leave the spray can, but thirty-plus years after the Montreal Protocol, stratospheric ozone levels are dropping. Scientists estimate that if the trend continues, the ozone layer will recover by 2060. By eliminating chlorofluorocarbons, the treaty also keeps 170 million tons (154 million t) of CO_2 out of the atmosphere annually.

A WORLDWIDE EFFORT

Fresh off the success of the Montreal Protocol, policymakers again turned to the larger issue of climate change. In March 1988, a bipartisan group of forty-two senators urged Reagan to build on the success of the Montreal Protocol by joining with the Soviet Union (a group of republics that included Russia) in an international treaty to address climate change. By May the US and the Soviet Union pledged to cooperate to address the issue.

Momentum built that summer, when Jim Hansen, a scientist who had worked to move politicians to act for over a decade, said this in a Senate hearing, "The greenhouse effect has been detected, and it is changing our climate now." Newspapers across the country took up the cry. Public awareness of the issue climbed to 68 percent. And a candidate in the 1988 presidential election made the greenhouse effect a campaign constant. That candidate was Republican George H. W. Bush.

In November, Bush won. Legislators closed out the year having considered thirty-two climate-related bills the previous twelve months. Among the successes, the bipartisan National Energy Policy Act of 1988 set goals of 2 percent energy use reduction per year until 2005, considered the possibility of a carbon tax, and urged the nation to work toward an international agreement on climate by 1992. As 1989 approached and Washington, DC, prepared for a new president, memos circulated discussing the need for immediate action on the climate. One memo said, "While it is clear that we need to know more about climate change, prudence dictates that we also begin to weigh impacts and possible responses. We simply cannot wait—the costs of inaction will be too high."

After a decade of study and debate, the nation and the world seemed poised to take significant action on climate change. In November 1989, delegates from sixty nations headed to Noordwijk in the Netherlands to participate in an international meeting to pave the way for an international treaty. Anticipation ran high. The representatives from most nations had come to the meeting already planning to sign an agreement. The one notable exception was the United States.

Bush's enthusiasm for climate action on the campaign trail belied disinterest while in office. After his inauguration, he delegated climate discussions to his chief of staff, John Sununu, who had forbidden anyone in the administration without a scientific background to use the terms *climate change* and *global warming*. Sununu opposed binding action at the Noordwijk meetings and urged the US delegate, Allan Bromley, to obstruct any agreement. The US convinced Japan, Britain, and the Soviet Union to join in its opposition. Though both Democratic and Republican policymakers and politicians back home supported climate action, a handful of opponents were able to halt international progress despite a decade of bipartisan environmental and policy efforts.

"NEW" WORLD, OLD PROBLEM

Settlers arriving in North America from England left a country where ancient forest laws were enforced. These laws reserved hunting and harvest rights for wealthy and landed classes, with harsh penalties for a peasant hunter just trying to eat.

These early settlers also created land-use laws, but they largely ensured resources for the future and fair access for everyone. One early practice stipulated that 1 acre (0.4 ha) of trees was to be left for every 5 acres (2 ha) cut. When the trade in deerskins led to the depletion of herds in the late seventeenth century, hunting restrictions were enacted. These early laws focused on resource management—protecting timber and game for collective use in the future.

This idea of management prevailed into the early nineteenth century. But with the onset of the industrial revolution and the rise of cities, a new leisure class emerged. Wealthy factory owners and middle-class city dwellers turned to hunting, fishing, and recreational trips in the "wild" as relief from the din of urban life. While industrial and human waste increasingly sullied land and water near factories, wealthy industrialists used their influence to squash laws intended to curtail polluting activities. Meanwhile, in the rural areas they used for recreation, land-use laws crept back toward the English model.

For example, in the late nineteenth century, fish populations in New England had been decimated by industrial pollution. Efforts to restore these populations initially focused on species used by local people for food. These efforts quickly gave way to stocking fish species favored by out-of-town anglers. Fishing and hunting seasons emerged, as did restrictions on equipment, but these policies favored sport hunters and anglers. Local residents who hunted and fished for their livelihoods increasingly found themselves at the wrong end of the law when trying to provide for their families.

Racial and class disparities began to emerge. While game animals taken by recreational hunters were viewed as appropriate, individuals hunting songbirds, opossums, groundhogs, and other "nongame" species to feed their families were viewed with disdain. In 1913 William Hornaday, the New York Zoological Society director, wrote, "Italians in the east, Hungarians in Pennsylvania, and Austrians in Minnesota . . . it seems absolutely certain that all members of the lower classes of southern Europe are a dangerous menace to our wildlife."

African Americans in the South and American Indians in the West were the target of similar comments and attempts to regulate their activities. A 1909

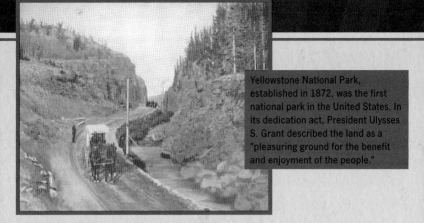

Yellowstone National Park, established in 1872, was the first national park in the United States. In its dedication act, President Ulysses S. Grant described the land as a "pleasuring ground for the benefit and enjoyment of the people."

issue of *Recreation* magazine included this line: "The pot-hunting negro has all the skill of the Indian, has more industry in his loafing, and kills without pity and without restraint."

"White Indians" in the West—rural subsistence hunters and farmers—were viewed with the same disdain. The militarization of such places as Yellowstone National Park, with limited entrances, guard cabins, and careful recording of all entries and exits, was enacted to limit the activities of local residents and to preserve the park for out-of-town recreation seekers.

Why does this matter a hundred years later? Because many early conservation groups, such as the Sierra Club and the Audubon Society, had strong ties to the racist and classist viewpoints of recreational hunters and anglers. They believed that poor and minority communities were directly responsible for declining wildlife numbers. In a March 9, 2017, blog post, the Sierra Club's first black president, Aaron Mair, wrote, "Few Sierrans realize that race, population eugenics, and 'natural order' were critical features and values of our founders and naturalist societies of the late nineteenth and twentieth centuries, which largely blamed environmental degradation on developing and non-European populations." This history was part of the reason minority communities worried that Earth Day would draw attention away from their concerns.

When the environmental justice movement began in the late twentieth century, activists reached out to mainstream environmental groups for help addressing their concerns. The mainstream groups declined. Instead, they continued to focus exclusively on issues that were priorities in white communities, ignoring basic quality of life issues such as the lack of clean water, lead paint, and increased air pollution faced by poor communities. Though many groups have worked hard in recent years to repair these relationships, the specter of prejudice still hangs over the legacy of the environmental movement.

MUDDYING THE WATERS

Prior to the 1990s, the science of climate change was clear—there was no "other side." Evidence had been building since mid-century, and the Department of Energy's work in the 1970s was definitive. *There was no controversy about whether climate change was real, only about what could be done about it.* Fixing the greenhouse effect would require the entire globe to alter business and energy practices.

Inaction wasn't due to disagreement about the reality of climate change but rather inertia. Fixing the problem wouldn't be cheap. Entire industries would be upended or fade away. Every hearing, meeting, commission—anything—came back to the same conclusion: changing the fundamentals of the world's economy seemed insurmountable.

The solid science and inevitability of regulation alarmed impacted industries. As the 1980s waned, the American Petroleum Institute created a lobbying organization called the Global Climate Coalition. The US Chamber of Commerce and coal, electric, and automobile companies joined the coalition's efforts. They began to seek out scientists who expressed skepticism about any aspect of climate change, offering $2,000 for opinion pieces for the media.

Over the next decade, the coalition spent millions to inject disinformation into the climate policy deliberations. Its paid campaigns suggested that climate science wasn't well understood and that humanity's role in climate change was

WE ARE ALL ENVIRONMENTALISTS

In 1990 a poll showed 70 percent of Americans considered themselves environmentalists. Though disagreement existed in specific areas over various regulations, concern for Earth continued across party lines and geographic regions.

uncertain. Joining the coalition were coordinated efforts from industry-supported conservative think tanks, foundations, and politicians engaged in broader antienvironmental efforts. After Republicans won big in the 1994 congressional elections, their leadership joined efforts to debunk peer-reviewed science and advance the views of nonpeer-reviewed researchers.

Decades of incontrovertible evidence suddenly became debatable. The public began to express skepticism that climate change was real. Politicians from both parties, mirroring the doubts of their constituents, urged caution and further study.

The Global Climate Coalition's biggest victory in its efforts to muddy the waters came in 1997. The group spent $13 million in opposition to the Kyoto Treaty, a worldwide effort to reduce greenhouse gas emissions by 5 percent. Before the delegates even met, the Senate voted 95–0 in opposition to any kind of binding treaty. By the 2000 presidential election, the two leading candidates provided a study in contrast. Instead of agreeing that climate change was an issue but disagreeing about how to solve it, Al Gore called for urgent action while George W. Bush challenged the idea that climate change even exists.

The coalition disbanded in 2002, but the damage was done. Public trust in the work of climate scientists was irreparably harmed. Conservative media, talk show personalities, and celebrities constantly called the science into question and mocked policy intended to address the issue. Doing nothing became an acceptable option, because perhaps the problem didn't really exist.

FROM CRACK TO CREVASSE

After 2000 the divide only deepened. Acrimony over the climate debate solidified opposition not just to climate action but also to environmental policy. Steady corporate opposition to environmental regulations and ongoing frustration in rural communities with "big government" interference created additional obstacles to progress. The number of Americans self-identifying as environmentalists dropped from 78 percent of both Republicans and Democrats to 56 percent of Democrats and 27 percent of Republicans in 2016. Rather than being a term that Republican presidents Ronald Reagan and George H. W. Bush insisted applied to them, the word *environmentalist* had become synonymous with "liberal" and "Democrat."

Party line divisions meant that more than ever, steps toward environmental protections depended upon which party is in power. The George W. Bush (2001–2009) Republican presidency saw widespread rollbacks of regulations. The Bush administration cut funds for environmental cleanup; opened wilderness to mining, logging, and drilling; and cut back on EPA enforcement. But most damaging were overt and covert attempts to downplay and obscure scientific data supporting the immediacy and urgency of climate change. For example, former EPA officials accused Vice President Dick Cheney of stripping six pages of testimony given by Dr. Julie Gerberding, director of the Centers for Disease Control and Prevention. It outlined the dangers to human health posed by climate change.

In contrast, Obama's eight years in the White House (2009–2017) saw a complete reversal, with emphasis on climate science and advances on a range of environmental issues. But Obama's failure to win the support of Congress for most of his two terms in office meant his ability to act was limited to executive action and regulatory efforts. Nevertheless, the Obama administration made significant progress in several areas, most notably creating the Waters

IT'S NEVER ALL OR NOTHING

The range of issues dropped under the heading "environment" are extremely varied and complex. An administration widely seen as hostile to environmental protection often moves forward on some issues. And an administration openly committed to protecting the environment sometimes makes missteps. George W. Bush's administration made significant progress reducing diesel emissions. Bush also set aside almost 200,000 square miles (518,000 sq. km) of the Pacific Ocean as marine monuments, which bans fishing and limits mining and drilling.

While Obama worked to further environmental protections, his administration's response to Flint, Michigan's water crisis, in which officials failed to correct preventable lead contamination, was often criticized as ineffective. Activists also felt Obama failed to protect vulnerable communities, especially minorities, from the environmental effects of fracking and drilling.

of the United States rule in 2015, which extended Clean Water Act regulation to most bodies of water in the US, including smaller streams and lakes.

The Obama administration also blocked the planned Keystone XL pipeline. The pipeline, slated to run from Alberta to Nebraska, carries tar sands oil. The extraction creates "up to three times more global warming pollution than does producing the same quantity of conventional crude." Many environmental groups considered the Obama administration's opposition to this pipeline project a key step in addressing climate change. Obama also created the Clean Power Plan and expanded Papahānaumokuākea Marine National Monument, a marine sanctuary in Hawaii established during the Bush administration, to 582,578 square miles (1.5 million sq. km).

President Obama visited the Papahānaumokuākea Marine National Monument in September, 2016.

Amid the push and pull of bitterly divided politics in the United States, world efforts to create a climate agreement moved forward. More than twenty-five years after failed efforts in Noordwijk, negotiations between the US, China, and 185 other nations plus 120 smaller entities, such as states, provinces, and cities, produced the Paris Climate Agreement in 2015. The agreement established that participating countries agree to try to reduce their CO_2 emissions and to report their emissions regularly. Experts review the reporting to prevent cheating. Although the agreement is nonbinding—having no penalties for missing targets—it was a huge accomplishment for all nations involved.

FULL FRONTAL ASSAULT

In 2016 the campaign between Democrat Hillary Clinton and Republican Donald Trump captured the world's attention. Donald Trump portrayed himself as the champion of the downtrodden

YOUTH CLIMATE LAWSUIT

On September 10, 2015, a group of twenty-one young people, aged eleven to twenty-two, filed suit against the federal government in the US District Court in Oregon. The suit contends that the government has known of the risks posed by climate change for over fifty years, yet has continued to "permit, authorize, and subsidize fossil fuel extraction, development, consumption and exportation." The suit further alleges that failure to curtail this industry has "infringed on Plaintiffs' fundamental constitutional rights to life, liberty, and property."

The federal government, along with the fossil fuel industry, immediately and repeatedly moved to have the case dismissed. Their efforts failed, and a trial was set for February 5, 2018, though the fossil fuel industry defendants were removed from the case. As the trial date approached, the Trump administration redoubled its efforts to block the case, which delayed the trial. A new date was set for October 29, 2018. The federal government continued to evade a trial. It used a rarely deployed tactic, a writ of mandamus, which seeks to have a higher court overrule a lower court even before the case ends. The Supreme Court temporarily stopped the case but ultimately decided not to dismiss the suit.

In early 2019, the youth climate lawsuit continued the fight to bring its case to trial. On March 1, 2019, supporters filed amicus curiae briefs—legal declarations of support for the case. Writers of the fifteen briefs included members of the US Congress, medical doctors, religious groups, and over thirty-two thousand people under twenty-five. On April 4, Aji Piper, one of the plaintiffs in the suit, testified before the inaugural hearing of the US House of Representatives' Select Committee on the Climate Crisis. As of mid-2019, a decision on whether the case could proceed was still pending.

Aji Piper urged lawmakers to address the climate crisis during a hearing of the House Select Committee on the Climate Crisis in April 2019.

American dream, trampled by interference from outsiders and burdensome government policies. He repeatedly referred to climate change as a hoax and insisted that "the concept of global warming was created by and for the Chinese in order to make U.S. manufacturing non-competitive." Clinton, meanwhile, promised to continue environmental policies created under the Obama administration and to help the country meet its commitments under the Paris Climate Agreement.

Trump won the election and took office January 20, 2017. His administration immediately went to work to gut environmental policy. Initially, the Trump administration took a page from Ronald Reagan, appointing industry insiders who had long fought environmental regulation to cabinet-level posts in agencies such as the EPA and the Department of the Interior. But while Reagan saw federal environmental laws as government overreach that hurt the economy, he did not question the need for regulatory efforts to benefit human health. He did not attack the science behind environmental lawmaking, only the federal government's involvement in enacting and enforcing regulation. And when the economic benefits of an environmental regulation outweighed the costs, such as with chlorofluorocarbon regulations, Reagan supported them.

The Trump administration not only questioned the science upon which environmental regulations are based—evidence accumulated over years of scientific study collected under administrations of both parties—it actively sought to undermine and obfuscate the data. The administration removed references to climate change from government websites, including the White House, the EPA, and the Department of Energy.

Trump's assault on all environmental regulations began immediately. Days after his inauguration, Trump OK'd the Keystone XL and Dakota Access pipelines. In the Trump administration's first

AFTER EARTH DAY— KEEPING FARMWORKERS SAFE

Fifty years after farmworkers banded together to demand safer working conditions and fair pay, the EPA announced protections against unsafe pesticide use. Prior to this change, farmworkers were exempt from pesticide rules and safeguards that protected workers in other sectors.

The EPA ruling extends safeguards that some workers had won through labor negotiations to all two million US farmworkers. The ruling will likely significantly reduce the number of pesticide-related poisonings, which was from ten thousand to twenty thousand a year in 2015.

United Farm Workers president Arturo Rodriguez said about the announcement, "Our families and communities will now be able to work with reassurance that the work they are doing will not unknowingly harm themselves or their families. It's been a long time coming, but it has come today."

Pesticide exposure has been a major concern for farmworkers for decades.

two years, it began to undo the Waters of the United States rule and reversed a ban on lead ammunition on federal land—a rule designed in part to protect the rare California condor. The administration reversed rules to improve tracking of methane and other pollutants. Efforts to scrap the Clean Power Plan began. The administration removed thousands of acres from national monuments and opened up millions of acres for offshore oil and gas leases. Budgets for climate monitoring were slashed. Provisions of the Endangered Species Act came under threat. And on June 1, 2017, the Trump administration pulled the United States out of the Paris Climate Agreement. As the fiftieth anniversary of Earth Day approached, its cultural legacy remained undisputed, but its legislative legacy was increasingly under fire.

SUCCESSES ACHIEVED BY THE MODERN ENVIRONMENTAL MOVEMENT AFTER THE FIRST EARTH DAY

AIR QUALITY

- The entire nation meets air quality standards for carbon monoxide, and most of the nation meets standards for airborne lead pollution.

- From 1970 to 2017, emissions of six common pollutants—ozone, lead, carbon monoxide, nitrogen oxide, sulfur dioxide, and particulate matter—dropped by an average of 73 percent.

WATER QUALITY

- Federal, state, and local governments have made significant progress toward protecting US waters. No longer are the nation's rivers, lakes, and oceans dumping points for waste.

- A team of researchers scoured available data from 240,000 water quality monitoring sites over thirty-nine years and found that pollution had dropped in most locations.

WASTE MANAGEMENT

- In 2015 Americans recycled 34.7 percent of their waste, up from 6.6 percent in 1970.

- Around five hundred thousand highly toxic Superfund sites have been cleaned up. Parks, neighborhoods, and wildlife habitat thrive in once contaminated areas.

PESTICIDES AND CHEMICALS

- In 1972 the Federal Environmental Pesticide Control Act required that new pesticides undergo extensive testing to determine their environmental and human health impact.

- Later updates to the law set requirements for allowed pesticide residue on food.

ENDANGERED SPECIES

- DDT was banned in 1972, leading the way to remarkable recoveries for affected wildlife species.

- Of the 1,465 animals and 947 plant species listed as endangered or threatened under the Endangered Species Act, 99 percent are still around as of 2018.

CHAPTER 7

A NEW RESOLVE

Fifty years after the first Earth Day, one might be experiencing déjà vu. Daily reminders of just how bad things are flood television, print news, and social media. In many respects, progress on environmental issues seems to have stalled, and political and ideological divides seem set in stone. But a quick glance at headlines or a scroll through Twitter debates doesn't tell the whole story. Everyday acts of protest, simple gestures of concern, and tenacious work toward progress continue. Individuals and groups quietly help the planet—sometimes the alliances are surprising.

UNLIKELY PARTNERSHIPS

On September 17, 2015, after years of meetings and negotiations, Republican Chris Gibson (NY) introduced a resolution in the US House of Representatives that called on members to start working on climate change solutions. Twelve other Republican lawmakers joined in supporting the resolution, which urged House members to work "constructively, using our tradition of American ingenuity, innovation, and exceptionalism, to create and support economically viable, and broadly supported private and public solutions."

A few months later, on February 1, 2016, Florida representatives Carlos Curbelo (R) and Ted Deutch (D) formed the Climate Solutions Caucus, a bipartisan group of lawmakers that meets regularly to find solutions for climate change. The group's commitment to bipartisanship is so strong, members are admitted only in pairs—one Republican and one Democrat. A congressional caucus is a group of members that meets together to pursue common goals. The Climate Solutions Caucus's goal is to "educate members on economically viable options to reduce climate risk and protect our nation's economy, security, infrastructure, agriculture, water supply, and public safety."

In a sharply divided country, progress is slow and victories are few. The caucus did achieve a victory on July 13, 2017. When Republicans in the House of Representatives attempted to reverse regulations that require the Department of Defense to analyze the effects of climate change on the military, most of the caucus's Republican members joined Democrats to defeat it. The group also defeated efforts to remove language from the same bill that recognizes climate change as a "direct threat" to the country's national security.

Thirteen of the caucus's Republican members also joined Democrats to protect an Obama-era rule that requires the EPA to track and repair methane leaks resulting from extraction of natural gas. Methane traps twenty-five times more heat than CO_2. Though the attempt failed—the amendment that denied funding for this rule passed—the Climate Solutions Caucus has demonstrated that efforts to reach across party lines and work together are still ongoing.

These bipartisan efforts are not limited to Congress. In September 2018, Republican and Democratic governors from sixteen states and Puerto Rico joined the governments of Mexico and Canada to announce new efforts to combat climate change. These states are part of the US Climate Alliance. Member states pledged to honor the terms of the Paris Climate Agreement, despite that Trump pulled the United States out of it in 2017. By spring 2019, the number of participating states had risen to twenty-two.

The US Climate Alliance pledges to restrict the release of methane, in keeping with the Obama-era rule the Climate Solutions Caucus tried and failed to protect at the national level. The governors also pledge to create policies that will stem the costs of solar panel construction, which have increased since Trump imposed import tariffs on solar panels in early 2018. They also plan to study how carbon is stored in ecosystems and soil and to understand how land use might offset carbon emissions. Finally, the governors commit to spending $1.4 billion on electric car infrastructure.

According to Governor Jay Inslee (D-WA), this determination to move forward despite national setbacks is "important, right now, for both the nation's vision and its mental health. Trump can't stop us in the state. He can't stop us from having a clean energy fund. He can't stop me from moving forward to incentivize electric cars. He can't stop us from continuing with our renewable portfolio standards. And that's an important statement—he can tweet til the cows come home, but he can't stop us from adopting statewide policies."

TOADS AND WHEELS

Efforts to find creative partnerships on environmental issues aren't limited to addressing climate change. Under lonely desert skies in western Nevada, a partnership between a landowner and the Fish & Wildlife Service is creating opportunities for recreation and conservation. David Spicer's 320 acres (129 ha) near Beatty, Nevada, have become a destination for Tough Mudder endurance racers, Boy Scouts, and regional cultural events. He hopes to expand his land's recreational offerings to include opportunities for mountain climbers, as well as trails for mountain bikers, runners, and horseback riders.

HEALING THE RIFT

On Monday, September 27, 1982, police arrested Walter E. Fauntroy, Washington, DC's delegate to the US Congress, along with about 120 other people. The charges were impeding traffic and resisting arrest. Fauntroy and others had protested by laying in the road to block dump trucks carrying waste to a toxic landfill, which the State of North Carolina had decided to put in Warren County. Opponents of the landfill contended that the area was chosen because of its majority-black population.

The protesters lost the battle, and the toxic waste landfill went ahead. Even so, the civil action seemed to be the beginning of an organized fight for environmental justice. After participating in the protest, Fauntroy went on to confirm that toxic sites were indeed more likely to be near African American neighborhoods in at least three southeastern states.

Subsequent studies over the last fifty years continued to confirm that independent of income, people of color were far more likely to live in areas with higher environmental contamination. During that time, majority-white conservation and environmental groups have often failed to support environmental justice efforts.

This began to change in the 1990s, when environmental justice leaders publicly called upon mainstream groups such as the Sierra Club and the Natural Resources Defense Council to address their racial bias. Though change has been slow, these groups have acknowledged past failings and have committed to address them. For example, the Sierra Club elected Aaron Mair, its first African American president, in 2015. During his tenure, the group adopted a diversity statement and established its first chapter in Puerto Rico. And Bill Clinton signed Executive Order 12898—Federal Actions to Address Environmental Justice in Minority Population and Low-Income Populations—in 1994. The order requires federal agencies to consider environmental justice issues when making policy decisions. However, much work still lies ahead. A 2018 EPA study concluded that communities of color still face higher levels of environmental contaminates than their neighbors.

Aaron Mair has been a member of the Sierra Club since 1999.

Recreational land users have not always been sympathetic to efforts to protect wildlife habitat, but Spicer is trying to protect threatened Amargosa toads, which live on his property. The toads' habitat is limited to 10 miles (16 km) of the Amargosa River and a scattering of other sites in the area. Their extremely limited range, or home habitat, makes them exceptionally vulnerable to habitat loss due to ranching, mining, and recreational activities.

Amargosa toads live in a small area along the Amargosa River in Nevada.

Spicer and his nonprofit Saving Toads thru Off-road Racing, Ranching, and Mining in Oasis Valley believes that saving the toad and protecting economic opportunities for people aren't mutually exclusive. The nonprofit hopes to "demonstrate that the land use necessary to serve the needs of Civilization can be balanced to serve the needs of the Environment. That the 'Amargosa Toad' is benefitted by these actions not victimized." Spicer and his nonprofit, with help from the Fish and Wildlife Service, restored eleven springs, providing toad habitat through the hot, dry Nevada summers. They also improved 1 mile (1.6 km) of river habitat. In all, 57 acres (23 ha) of toad habitat have been created or enhanced, creating more areas of open water that last long enough into the summer for tadpoles to develop into toads.

Thanks to Spicer's efforts and that of others in the area, the Amargosa toad's population has increased. As of 2010, these modest gains have kept the toad off the US Fish and Wildlife Service's endangered species list.

FINDING COMMON GROUND

In Georgia an unlikely partnership has formed to protect the gopher tortoise. These reptiles grow to about 15 inches (38 cm) long and weigh between 8 to 15 pounds (3.6 to 6.8 kg). They are considered a keystone species—a species that two hundred other species, including indigo snakes, frogs, mice, foxes, skunks, lizards, and owls, depend upon for their deep burrows to survive.

As humans fanned out into gopher tortoise habitat to farm, log, and build houses, golf courses, shopping malls, and factories, populations of this important species plummeted. During the Great Depression (1929–1942), people also hunted for the tortoises for food, leading to the nickname Hoover's chickens. Because gopher tortoises reproduce so slowly, the species has had a difficult time bouncing back. Low population numbers make the tortoise a candidate for listing as a federal threatened or endangered species. If the species is listed, human activities on public and private land would be severely curtailed. Landowners and businesses would face land use restrictions and rising costs.

To avoid the restrictions and costs that would accompany an ESA listing, businesses and government agencies have joined conservation groups to help the tortoise. Georgia Power is restoring the longleaf pine forest at its Edwin I. Hatch Nuclear Plant and considering the tortoise as it manages vegetation on the property. The company also hosts scientists who study the tortoises. Conservation groups working with businesses and agencies raise young tortoises until they are a certain size

Gopher tortoises face many threats to their survival, but the greatest are habitat destruction and predation.

before releasing them in suitable habitat to give them a better chance to survive. They also locate populations of tortoises on private land and educate landowners about how to protect them.

Doug Miell, a Georgia Chamber of Commerce consultant, said this about the partnership, "There's always a perception that business and industry and conservation groups are at loggerheads, that we don't agree on anything. This is a good example of where we can come together to demonstrate that, hey, we might be looking at it from different sides, but the outcome is the same."

WHAT HAPPENED TO EARTH DAY?

Earth Day continues around the country, largely with no direction from a central organization. Travel to communities and schools across the nation on April 22, and you are likely to find some kind of commemoration, such as environmental fairs with tree planting events and face painting booths, litter control efforts, and ecumenical services held by church groups.

Some complain that contemporary Earth Day events have become too feel-good—that they make people feel good about doing something while having little real impact. There may be some truth to this

SENATOR NELSON HONORED FOR ENVIRONMENTAL EFFORTS

Gaylord Nelson died on July 3, 2005, at the age of eighty-nine. He lived to see thirty-five Earth Days and watched the commemoration spread around the world. In 1995 President Bill Clinton awarded him the Presidential Medal of Honor for his lifelong work to protect the environment.

assertion. No one would suggest that face painting and tree planting have the political punch of the first Earth Day. But they are a way to affirm to participants that these issues matter and to pass that concern along to their children and grandchildren.

Over the decades, some activists have mounted coordinated efforts to sustain the event. In 1990 Denis Hayes and others founded Earth Day Network. That year the organization worked to make Earth Day a global event. As of the mid-2010s, the organization partners with fifty thousand individuals and groups around the world in over 190 countries, participating in educational programs, consumer campaigns, and policy discussions. Earth Day's international celebration has grown from about two hundred million people a year worldwide in 1990 to over one billion people a year.

Earth Day Network runs more than two dozen individual campaigns to spark environmental action worldwide. It has launched sister programs in India and China, the world's two most populous nations. Its actions include registering voters concerned about climate change, preparing environmental education materials for schools and churches, supporting women in environmental leadership, and planting trees in cities and schoolyards worldwide.

April 22, 2020, is Earth Day's fiftieth birthday. On this occasion, Earth Day Network launched Earth Challenge 2020, a global citizen science initiative. The ongoing challenge recruits citizen scientists from around the world to collect data on air and water quality, pollution, and human health. The group hopes to collect one billion data points. They believe these will provide a full picture of the state of our worldwide environment.

Earth Day Network also sponsored a monthlong volunteer program: the Great Global Cleanup. K–12 students, teachers, and community members worldwide removed trash from roadsides, communities, and natural areas. Working with partners, they planted one tree for every human on the planet—an estimated 7.8 billion trees.

A LASTING LEGACY

When planning the first Earth Day, Nelson wanted to send a loud and clear message to Congress that people cared about the environment and demanded that they act to protect it. He succeeded. But more important, Nelson and all who have worked to protect the environment since hoped to make caring for the planet an integral part of American culture. Despite problems that feel insurmountable, the environmental movement will continue to succeed so long as people care enough to take action.

> Our goal is an environment of decency, quality, and mutual respect for all human beings and all other living creatures—an environment without ugliness, without ghettos, without poverty, without discrimination, without hunger, and without war. Our goal is a decent environment in its broadest, deepest sense.
>
> —Gaylord Nelson, Milwaukee, April 21, 1970

WHAT ABOUT PROTESTS AND DEMONSTRATIONS?

Protests and demonstrations can be an effective tool in political action, but by themselves they accomplish little. One of the reasons Earth Day 1970 left such a lasting legacy was that the actions people took on April 22 occurred in the context of ongoing activism. Though it may have been a one-and-done event for some people, many participants continued to work for change long after Earth Day ended. They wrote letters. They changed their own behavior. And most important, they voted for politicians who shared their determination to protect the environment. This sustained action ultimately made the difference.

MAKING IT PERSONAL

Books like this always include nice lists of things you can do to save Earth. They often feel hollow, because the truth is, no one person, group, or state can save the world alone. Nelson understood this when he created Earth Day. To save Earth requires collective national and international action. So what can one person do?

VOTE!

Voting is the one collective action the citizens of this country can do every year. Concerned citizens lifting their collective voices have challenged even the most powerful corporate interests.

People have all kinds of reasons for not voting. Probably the most common is that one vote won't matter. But when 54 percent of voters sit out an election, that is another kind of collective action. (Only 46.1 percent of eligible voters under thirty voted in the 2016 presidential election.) Voting is the most effective personal action any person can take.

ENGAGE IN THE POLITICAL PROCESS

Another important step to help the planet is to engage in the political process beyond voting. Call and write letters to your representatives in local, state, and national government. Let them know how you feel about the issues. Do it often.

Support candidates who share your environmental values. Do it in ways that are comfortable for you. Some people like to stand on a street corner and wave a sign, and some don't. You can find many ways to get involved. Post a sign. Wear a pin. Make a donation. Knock on doors. Make calls. Check with a candidate's campaign office to see how you can help. Now that you're involved, consider running for office yourself in the future.

THREE MORE THINGS

None of these other actions will make as much difference as voting, but turn the page to read about a few more things you can do that will make a difference over time.

BUY LESS

You don't need a carbon footprint calculator to tell you that whether you buy an organic cotton shirt or a regular cotton shirt, you still have an impact on the world. In fact, a recent study demonstrated that people who buy green products have similar carbon footprints to those who don't. The problem? Producing and shipping a product consumes natural resources, whether the product's green or not.

This doesn't mean you shouldn't buy environmentally responsible products when you can (do a little digging to make sure the green claims add up), but a better option is to consider carefully if you need the product. Buy only what you really need. Buy as durable as you can afford. Use the product for as long as possible. Repeat.

EAT LESS BEEF

A 2017 study found that if Americans eliminated beef from their diets—just beef, no other animal products—that we would reach about half our targeted reductions in greenhouse gas emissions.

A 2018 study out of the University of Oxford gathered data from 38,700 farms, as well as processors and packagers in all parts of the food industry. It, too, found that beef production ranked the worst for emissions, followed by all other animal products. So reducing the consumption of all animal products, but especially beef, makes a huge difference.

AIM FOR ZERO WASTE

A zero-waste lifestyle aims for an empty trash can every day. That sounds daunting for most Americans, but you don't have to start all at once. One strategy is to reduce the number of items coming into your life. This includes buying less, as mentioned previously, but also includes paying attention to such things as how much throwaway packaging a product includes. When you buy something, try to buy items that can be reused, recycled, or both. By bringing in only items that you need or will enjoy most *and* that can be reused or recycled after they are no longer needed, you can reduce the amount of waste.

Some zero-waste followers have achieved astounding success—reducing their yearly trash haul to a plastic bag full of bits and bobs. That takes time and effort to achieve, and sometimes money. Not everyone has the ability or the resources to go that far. But even a modest effort can have a significant impact.

A THOUSAND OTHER THINGS

You can do a thousand tiny things to help the environment every day. Turn off the lights. Take the bus. Recycle. Buy sustainable seafood. Use a reusable bottle. Ditch the straws. Just like voting, it feels as if none of these things makes much difference. Maybe they don't, individually, but as one vote added to another added to another makes all the difference, so, too, does one action added to another action. Do one thing. Do it often. Share it with others. Because doing something small is always better than doing nothing.

GLOSSARY

AP newswire: a cooperative news service owned by its contributing news sources—newspapers and television and radio stations across the country. Any other contributing news source can use stories contributed by member news sources and by AP staffers.

Bakkan Formation oil fields: a large area of oil and natural gas deposits in parts of the United States (North Dakota and Montana) and Canada (Saskatchewan and Manitoba)

benzene: a common chemical used in the manufacturing of products from plastics to detergents. It is also found in oil and gasoline. Benzene exposure is known to cause cancer in humans.

bipartisan: typically used to describe legislation or other efforts supported by members of both major US political parties

carbon monoxide: a gas formed when carbon burns incompletely. It is toxic and is present in vehicle exhaust.

DDT (dichloro-diphenyl-trichloroethane): an insecticide initially developed in the 1940s to combat malaria, typhus, and other diseases carried by insects

environmental impact statement: a document required by federal law that assesses the impact, either positive or negative, of a proposed action on the environment

greenwashing: an activity by a company to make its practices appear more environmentally friendly than they are

hydrogen sulfide: a toxic gas generated by oil burning and refining. It smells like rotten eggs.

methane: a gaseous hydrocarbon that is the main component of natural gas

mitigate: to make an outcome less severe. In an environmental context, *mitigate* often refers to activities undertaken to offset the known impacts of an activity. For example, Steigerwald Lake National Wildlife Refuge near the Columbia Gorge in Washington State was established to offset, or mitigate, habitat losses due to the construction of an additional powerhouse at Bonneville Lock and Dam farther upstream

obfuscate: to make something harder to understand or less clear

ozone: an oxygen molecule containing three oxygen atoms. In the upper atmosphere, it absorbs radiation. In the lower atmosphere, it is a harmful pollutant.

smog: originally, a combination of the words *fog* and *smoke*, the word *smog* refers to any visible air pollution, the source of which varies by location

supersonic: faster than the speed of sound

SOURCE NOTES

7   Robert Sollen, quoted in *Sand, Sun, Oil, and Gas*, YouTube video, 28:02, posted by Earth Alert!, 2015, November 16, 2015, 5:35, https://www.youtube .com/watch?v=OsivwmPwuY0.

7   Mike McCorkle, quoted in "Trailer: Stories of the Spill," YouTube video, 6:00, posted by Earth Alert!, 2011, July 11, 2011, 2:00 https://www.youtube .com/watch?v=SDXqEk9W-Cw.

11 Fred Hartley, quoted in "Water Pollution—1969: Hearings before the United State Senate Committee on Public Works, Subcommittee on Air and Water Pollution, Ninety-First Congress, First Session, 1969" (Washington, DC: United States Government Printing Office, February 3–4, 1969), 342, https:// babel.hathitrust.org/cgi/pt?id=umn.31951d02137877k;view=1up;seq=9.

11 Fred Hartley, quoted in "Head of Union Oil Denies Remarks on Loss of Birds in Slick," *New York Times (1923-Current file)*, February 19, 1969, ProQuest.

11 Bud Bottoms, quoted in Kate Wheeling and Max Ufberg, "'The Ocean Is Boiling': The Complete History of the 1969 Santa Barbara Oil Spill," *Pacific Standard*, April 18, 2017, https://psmag.com/news/the-ocean-is-boiling-the -complete-oral-history-of-the-1969-santa-barbara-oil-spill.

12 Robert Sollen, *An Ocean of Oil: A Century of Political Struggle over Petroleum off the California Coast* (Juneau, AK: Denali, 1998), 51.

14 Sollen, 49.

15 Richard Nixon, quoted in Jim Byron, "RN's Response to the Santa Barbara Oil Spill," Richard Nixon Foundation, July 1, 2010, https://www .nixonfoundation.org/2010/07/rns-response-to-the-santa-barbara-oil-spill/.

15 Robert Easton, *Black Tide: The Santa Barbara Oil Spill and Its Consequences* (New York: Delacorte, 1972), 137.

20 Gaylord Nelson, quoted in Bill Christofferson, *The Man from Clear Lake: Earth Day Founder Senator Gaylord Nelson* (Madison: University of Wisconsin Press, 2004), 302.

21 Gaylord Nelson, quoted in Christofferson, *The Man from Clear Lake*, I.

21 Fred Dutton, "Prospectus for a National Teach In on Our Worsening Environment," accessed at *Gaylord Nelson and Earth Day*, University of Wisconsin, document archived in the Nelson Collection at the Wisconsin Historical Society, IV, http://www.nelsonearthday.net/docs/nelson_126-10 _dutton_prospectus_a.pdf.

22 Gaylord Nelson, quoted in Adam Rome, *The Genius of Earth Day: How a 1970 Teach-In Unexpectedly Made the First Green Generation* (New York: Hill and Wang, 2013), 57.

24 "Smog Here Nears the Danger Point; Patients Warned," *New York Times (1923–Current file),* November 25, 1966, ProQuest.

24 Roy Popkin, "Two Killer Smogs the Headlines Missed," *EPA Journal—Our Fragile Atmosphere: The Greenhouse Effect and Ozone Depletion,* 12, no. 10 (December 1986): 27–29, https://nepis.epa.gov/Exe/ZyPDF.cgi/93000EN0 .PDF?Dockey=93000EN0.PDF.

27 C. Seldon Morely, quoted in Steven V. Roberts, "Charge of Peril in Pesticides Adds Fuel to Coast Grape Strike," *New York Times (1923–Current file)*, March 16, 1969, ProQuest.

27 Francisco Mendoza, quoted in Roberts.

27 Cesar Chavez, quoted in Roberts.

28 Carl Stokes, quoted in Rome, *The Genius of Earth Day*, 143.

28 Freddie Mae Brown, quoted in David Hendin, "Black Environmentalists See Another Side of Pollution," accessed at *Gaylord Nelson and Earth Day*, University of Wisconsin, document archived in the Nelson Collection at the Wisconsin Historical Society, http://www.nelsonearthday.net/docs/nelson _157-4_enterprise_science_black_environmentalists013.pdf.

34 Brownie Carson, quoted in Beth Quimby, "Earth Day at 40: Mainers Remember Birth of a Movement," *Portland Press Herald*, April 21, 2010, https://www.pressherald.com/2010/04/21/mainers-remember-the-birth-of-a -movement_2010-04-21/.

35–36 Phillips McCandlish, "The Day the City Caught Its Breath," *New York Times (1923-Current file)*, April 23, 1970, ProQuest.

36 *Washington Post*, April 23, 1970, quoted in Rome, *The Genius of Earth Day*, 120.

37 Gaylord Nelson, "Partial Text for Senator Gaylord Nelson, Denver, Colo., April 22," accessed at *Gaylord Nelson and Earth Day*, University of Wisconsin, document archived in the Nelson Collection at the Wisconsin Historical Society, http://www.nelsonearthday.net/docs/nelson_26-18_ED_denver _speech_notes.pdf.

39 Nelson.

39 "Earth Day 1970 Part 1: Intro" (*CBS News with Walter Cronkite*), YouTube video, 3:21, posted by EarthWeek 1970, April 11, 2010, 1:18, https://www .youtube.com/watch?v=WbwC281uzUs.

40 *New York Daily News*, April 23, 1970, quoted in Rome, *The Genius of Earth Day*, 119.

41 Earth Day performer in St. Louis, quoted in Clark Randall and Jacqui Germain, "Environmental Racism in St. Louis," *New Inquiry*, January 27, 2017, https://thenewinquiry.com/environmental-racism-in-st-louis/.

44 Joan Saxe, quoted in Quimby, "Earth Day at 40."

45 Dorothy M. Bradley, "Dorothy Bradley Interview, September 29, 2009," *Bob Brown Oral History Project*, OH 396-062, ScholarWorks, University of Montana, 1:44, 2:55, 3:03, https://scholarworks.umt.edu/brown/6/.

46 Rome, *The Genius of Earth Day*, 164.

46 Rome, 264–265.

47 Chad Montrie, *A People's History of Environmentalism in the United States* (New York: Continuum International, 2011), 31.

47 Urban Woodbury, quoted in Mark Bushnell, "Then Again: When the Green Mountains Were Not so Green," *VTDigger*, July 15, 2008, https://vtdigger .org/2018/07/15/green-mountains-not-green/.

56 Melissa Denchak, "The Dirty Fight Over Canadian Tar Sands Oil," *NRDC*, December 31, 2105, https://www.nrdc.org/stories/dirty-fight-over-canadian -tar-sands-oil.

57 Sophia Manolis, "Sophia Manolis, 17-Year-Old Youth Climate Intervenor at Today's Rally," Facebook, October 28, 2018, https://www.facebook.com /watch/?v=245543376140446.

57 Youth Climate Intervenors, "Enbridge Announced to Their Shareholders Last Month that they won't be starting full construction until early 2020! . . ." Facebook, April 5, 2019, https://www.facebook.com/pg/ YouthClimateIntervenors/posts/?ref=page_internal.

58 Richard Nixon, quoted in "Nixon Promises Urgent Fight to End Pollution," *New York Times (1923-Current file)*, January 2, 1970, ProQuest.

58 Linda Luther, "The National Environmental Policy Act: Background and Implementation," CRS Report for Congress, Order Code RL33152, (Congressional Research Service, 16 November 2005), CRS-7, https://fas.org /sgp/crs/misc/RL33152.pdf.

59 Nixon, quoted in "Nixon Promises Fight."

62 Bill de Blasio, quoted in "New York City's Air Is Cleaner Than It Has Ever Been Since Monitoring Began," NYC, April 19, 2018, https://www1.nyc.gov /office-of-the-mayor/news/204-18/new-york-city-s-air-cleaner-it-has-ever -been-since-monitoring-began.

64 "Woodsy Owl Launches Anti-Pollution Campaign," press release, U.S. Department of Agriculture, September 15, 1971, pdf, available at Forest History Society, https://foresthistory.org/wp-content/uploads/2018/07 /Woodsy_Owl_press.pdf.

66 "A Neighborhood Fights Back (transcript)," Roots of Health Inequity, National Association of County and City Health Officials (NACCHO), accessed September 5, 2019, http://rootsofhealthinequity.org/west-harlem -story.php.

67 David Falconer, Documerica, US National Archives, 412-DA-12965, flickr, accessed September 5, 2019, https://www.flickr.com/photos/ usnationalarchives/4272463964.

73 Robert W. Cairns, letter to Senator Gaylord Nelson, April 2, 1970, accessed at *Gaylord Nelson and Earth Day*, University of Wisconsin, document archived in the Nelson Collection at the Wisconsin Historical Society, http://www.nelsonearthday.net/docs/nelson_6-28_business_leaders_ED _letters.pdf.

73 R. D. Kemplin, Letter to Senator Gaylord Nelson, April 2, 1970, accessed at *Gaylord Nelson and Earth Day*.

73 Robert F Testin, letter to Senator Gaylord Nelson, April 2, 1970, accessed at *Gaylord Nelson and Earth Day*.

76 Cal Black, quoted in Raymond Wheeler, "War on the Colorado Plateau," *High Country News*, September 12, 1988, https://s3.amazonaws.com/hcn -media/archive-pdf/1988_09_12_Wheeler.pdf.

77 "The Long Term Impact of Atmospheric Carbon Dioxide on Climate," JASON, Technical Report JSR-78-07, April 1979, 29, Google, https://fas.org /irp/agency/dod/jason/co2.pdf.

78 Jule G. Charney et al, "Carbon Dioxide and Climate: A Scientific Assessment," National Academy of Sciences, 1979, 17, https://www.nap .edu/catalog/12181/carbon-dioxide-and-climate-a-scientific-assessment.

79 Ronald Reagan, "Inaugural Address," *The American Presidency Project*, January 20, 1981, https://www.presidency.ucsb.edu/documents/inaugural -address-11.

81 Robert Walker, quoted in Rich, "Losing Earth: The Decade We Almost Stopped Climate Change," *New York Times Magazine*, August 1, 2018, https://www.nytimes.com/interactive/2018/08/01/magazine/climate-change -losing-earth.html.

82 James Hansen, quoted in Rich.

83 Frederick M. Bernthal, memorandum to Richard T. McCormack, under secretary-designate for economic affairs, United States Department of State, February 9, 1989, https://nsarchive2.gwu.edu/NSAEBB/NSAEBB536 -Reagan-Bush-Recognized-Need-for-US-Leadership-on-Climate-Change-in -1980s/documents/Document%208.pdf.

84 William Hornaday, "Our Vanishing Wildlife," 100, quoted in Chad Montrie, *A People's History of Environmentalism in the United States* (New York: Continuum Books, 2011), 44.

85 Forty-Second Congress of the United States of America, "Act Establishing Yellowstone National Park (1872)," National Park Service, July 13, 2018, https://www.nps.gov/yell/learn/management/yellowstoneprotectionact1872 .htm.

85 Charles Askins, "The South's Problem in Game Protection," *Recreation*, May 1909, quoted in Montrie, 47.

85 Aaron Mair, "A Deeper Shade of Green," Sierra Club, March 9, 2017, https:// www.sierraclub.org/change/2017/03/deeper-shade-green#.

89 Denchak, "Dirty Fight."

91 Juliana v. U.S., Case No.: 6:15-cv-01517-TC (United States District Court, District of Oregon-Eugene Division, 2015), https://static1.squarespace.com /static/571d109b04426270152febe0/t/57a35ac5ebbd1ac03847eece /1470323398409/YouthAmendedComplaintAgainstUS.pdf.

92 Donald Trump, quoted in Louis Jacobson, "Yes, Donald Trump Did Call Climate Change a Chinese Hoax," *PolitiFact*, June 3, 2016, https://www .politifact.com/truth-o-meter/statements/2016/jun/03/hillary-clinton/yes -donald-trump-did-call-climate-change-chinese-h/.

93 "Farm Workers Win Long-Fought Battle for Pesticide Work Protections under New EPA Rules," United Farmworkers, September 28, 2015, https:// ufw.org/Farm-workers-win-long-fought-battle-for-pesticide-worker -protections-under-new-EPA-rules/.

96–97 "CCL Applauds Republican Resolution Calling for Action on Climate Change," Citizens' Climate Lobby, September 17, 2015, https:// citizensclimatelobby.org/ccl-applauds-republican-resolution-calling-for -action-on-climate-change/.

97 "What Is the Climate Solutions Caucus," Citizens' Climate Lobby, (text changed following November 2018 election), https://citizensclimatelobby.org /climate-solutions-caucus/.

98 Jay Inslee, quoted in Robinson Meyer, "17 Bipartisan Governors Vow to Fight Climate Change—And President Trump," *Atlantic*, September 13, 2018, https://www.theatlantic.com/science/archive/2018/09/17-states-vow-to-fight -climate-change-with-new-policies/570172/.

100 "Our Goals." STORM-OV, accessed September 5, 2019, http://storm-ov.org /goals.html.

102 Doug Miell, quoted in Molly Samuel, "Business and Wildlife Groups Skip the Fight, Work Together to Save a Species," *NPR*, January 28, 2018, https:// www.npr.org/2018/01/28/578689174/business-and-wildlife-groups-skip-the -fight-work-together-to-save-a-species.

104 Gaylord Nelson, "Milwaukee Earth Day Speech," April 21, 1970, accessed at *Gaylord Nelson and Earth Day*, University of Wisconsin, document archived in the Nelson Collection at the Wisconsin Historical Society, http://www .nelsonearthday.net/video/vha593_nelsonearthday.php.

SELECTED BIBLIOGRAPHY

Brooks, Karl Boyd. *Before Earth Day: The Origins of American Environmental Law, 1945–1970*. Lawrence: University Press of Kansas, 2009.

Christofferson, Bill. *The Man from Clear Lake: Earth Day Founder Senator Gaylord Nelson*. Madison: University of Wisconsin Press, 2004.

Easton, Robert. *Black Tide: The Santa Barbara Oil Spill and Its Consequences*. New York: Delacorte, 1972.

"Gaylord Nelson and Earth Day." Nelson Institute for Environmental Studies. University of Wisconsin. Accessed September 5, 2019. http://www.nelsonearthday .net/index.php.

Montrie, Chad. *A People's History of Environmentalism in the United States*. New York: Continuum Books, 2011.

Rich, Nathaniel. "Losing Earth: The Decade We Almost Stopped Climate Change." *New York Times Magazine,* August 1, 2018. https://www.nytimes.com/interactive /2018/08/01/magazine/climate-change-losing-earth.html.

Rome, Adam. *The Genius of Earth Day: How a 1970 Teach-In Unexpectedly Made the First Green Generation*. New York: Hill and Wang, 2013.

Sollen, Robert. *An Ocean of Oil: A Century of Political Struggle over Petroleum off the California Coast*. Juneau, AK: Denali, 1998.

Wheeler, Raymond. "War on the Colorado Plateau." *High Country News*, September 12, 1988. https://s3.amazonaws.com/hcn-media/archive-pdf/1988_09_12_ Wheeler.pdf.

Wheeling, Kate, and Max Ufberg. "'The Ocean Is Boiling': The Complete History of the 1969 Santa Barbara Oil Spill." *Pacific Standard*, April 18, 2017. https:// psmag.com/news/the-ocean-is-boiling-the-complete-oral-history-of-the-1969 -santa-barbara-oil-spill.

FURTHER INFORMATION

Carson, Rachel. *Silent Spring*. Boston: Houghton Mifflin, 1962.
This environmental classic might be almost sixty years old, but it is still readable and relevant.

Communities for a Better Environment
http://www.cbecal.org/
If you're in California, find out how you can get involved with Communities for a Better Environment. Otherwise, the site has great ideas for actions you can take in your own community.

Earth Day Network
https://www.earthday.org/
The official website of the organization that coordinates Earth Day and other environmental actions around the world.

"Earth Day 1970 CBS News with Walter Cronkite (Full)." YouTube video, 3:21. Posted by Earthweek 1970, April 25, 2010. https://www.youtube.com/playlist?list =PL3480E41AA956A42B
This archival news footage from April 22, 1970, is a fascinating peek into the first Earth Day from the perspective of a news network coverage of the events.

Gulf Oil Spill
https://ocean.si.edu/conservation/pollution/gulf-oil-spill
This website from the Smithsonian covers the more recent *Deepwater Horizon* oil spill in 2010. It includes information about oil spills and their impact on the environment.

Indigenous Youth Council
https://indigenousyouth.org/
Find out more about the Indigenous Youth Council.

McGraw, Sally. *Living Simply: A Teen Guide to Minimalism*. Minneapolis: Twenty First Century Books, 2019.
Consuming less isn't a new concept. This book explores how living simply can* help you live better and protect Earth.

Mihaly, Christy. *Diet for a Changing Climate*. Minneapolis: Twenty First Century Books, 2018.
Learn more about how your food choices affect the climate and how our diets might change in the future to protect the planet.

"What Is Environmental Justice?" YouTube video. 1:56. Posted by NRDCflix, December 13, 2017. https://www.youtube.com/watch?v=fIu-AfQ0cBM.
This short video from the Natural Resources Defense Council gives a brief overview of the concept of environmental justice.

Youth Climate Lawsuit
https://www.youthvgov.org/
Follow the progress of *Juliana vs. U.S.* lawsuit.

Zero Hour
http://thisiszerohour.org/
Do you want to get involved in the youth climate movement? This is the place to start.

INDEX

activism, 53, 59–60, 67, 70, 81, 103–104
  fragmented, 17, 55
  by persons of color, 27, 40–41, 66, 85, 89
  youth, 31, 42, 56–57, 69, 91, 105–107
air quality, 31, 33, 35, 53, 55, 62, 66, 78, 85, 95, 103
American Indian nations, 85
  broken treaties, 50–51
  oil pipeline protests, 42, 50–51, 57
Army Corps of Engineers, 42, 52
arrests, 37, 99

beef production, 106
bipartisan initiatives, 25, 38, 82–83, 97
BPA, 68
Bradley, Dorothy, 45–46, 59
Bureau of Land Management (BLM), 75–76
Bush, George H. W., 88
  actions in office, 83
  campaign trail policies, 82–83
Bush, George W., 87–90

carbon dioxide, 65, 77–78, 81, 90
carbon monoxide, 24, 33, 35, 62, 95
car burials, 37, 61
Chavez, Cesar, 27
chemicals used in oil extraction, 31
chlorofluorocarbons (CFCs), 81–82, 92
civil rights movement, 19, 22, 26, 28–29, 36
Clean Air Coalition, 53
climate change, 42, 51, 72–94
  Charney report, 78
  congressional response, 80–81, 83, 87–89, 96–97
  global efforts, 81–83, 90, 97, 103
  misinformation, 86–88, 92
  paper trail, 94
  studies, 77–78, 80–81
Clinton, Bill, 99, 102
Clinton, Hillary Rodham, 90, 92
Coast Guard, 7
conservation and business partnerships, 43, 101–102
conservation groups, 26, 52, 58, 71, 85, 89–90, 99, 101–102, 105
  See also racism in conservation groups

corporate responses to Earth Day, 68, 72–73, 76, 88
cost-benefit analysis, 58, 79, 81, 92
Council on Environmental Quality, 54–55, 58, 77, 80
Cronkite, Walter, 39–40

Dakota Access Pipeline, 42, 92
  See also American Indian nations
DDT, 22, 46
  birds and, 23, 33, 71, 95
  food with, 33
  Silent Spring (Carson), 18
Dead Orange Parade, 37
drilling mud, 4, 7, 13
dumping pollutants, 8, 16, 33, 47–48, 99
Dutton, Fred, 20–22, 29

early environmental efforts, 47, 84
early environmental laws, 49
Earth Day, 28, 85
  effects on participants, 43–46, 53, 60, 64–65, 68–70
  fiftieth anniversary, 94, 96, 102–103
  first events, 30–32, 34–41, 61
  goals, 23–26
  naming, 21, 29
  staff, 21–22, 25–32
Earth Day Network, 103
Eco-Commando Force '70, 37
ecology centers, 64, 67
emissions, 62–63, 68, 78, 87, 89–90, 95, 98, 106
energy crisis of 1973, 67
Energy Star, 68
engine funerals, 37
environmentalist label, 72, 86, 88
environmental justice, 85, 99
Environmental Protection Agency (EPA), 54–59, 77, 80, 88, 92–93, 97, 99
everyday environmentalism, 43–44, 58–59, 62, 65, 67–70, 96

farmworkers, 27, 33, 93
Federal Land Policy and Management Act (FLPMA), 75–76
Fresh Kills landfill, 16, 65

Global Climate Coalition, 86–87
GOO!, 11–12
Great Lakes Water Quality Agreement, 74
greenhouse effect. *See* climate change
greenwashing, 68

Hartley, Fred, 11
Hayes, Denis, 26, 29, 36, 103
high school participation, 25–26, 30, 37–38,
    43, 56–57, 69
hunting, 46, 101
    discrimination, 50, 84–85
    regulation, 84–85

industrial waste, 8, 33, 34, 43, 47–49, 54–56,
    66, 84, 95, 99
infographics
    Disaster at Platform A, 6
    Environmental Concerns Prior to the First
        Earth Day, 33
    Santa Barbara oil spill, 13
    successes achieved by the modern
        environmental movement after the first
        Earth Day, 95

Keystone XL pipeline, 89, 92

landfills, 10, 16, 63, 65, 66, 99
laws passed after Earth Day
    Clean Air Act, 53, 55, 62, 73
    Clean Water Act, 55, 89
    Endangered Species Act, 55, 75, 94
    Federal Insecticide, Fungicide, and
        Rodenticide Act, 55
    Resource Conservation and Recovery Act,
        55
    See also Federal Land Policy and
        Management Act (FLPMA)
laws passed before Earth Day
    Air Pollution Control Act, 49
    Federal Water Pollution Control Act, 49
    Migratory Bird Treaty Act, 49
    Rivers and Harbors Appropriation Act,
        48–49
    Solid Waste Disposal Act, 49, 55
    Wilderness Act, 75, 77
    See also National Environmental Policy Act
lead, 28, 32–33, 41, 62, 80, 85, 89, 94–95
littering, 38, 46, 63–64, 102
lobbyists, 53, 59, 62, 73, 86–87

media coverage, 17, 19, 22–23, 39, 43, 54, 58,
    86–87
minority communities, 85
    disproportionate pollution effects, 27,
        40–42, 50, 61, 66, 89, 93, 99
    Earth Day participation, 28, 40–41, 43
Montreal Protocol, 81–82

National Environmental Policy Act (NEPA)
    creation, 26, 54–55
    legacy, 58
Nelson, Gaylord, 18–23, 25–26, 28–32, 39,
    53–54, 60, 72, 102, 104–105
New York City, 16, 65
    events, 30, 34–36, 70
    OneNYC plan, 62
    pollution levels, 24, 40, 62, 66

Obama, Barack, 42, 89–90, 92, 97–98
offshore drilling, 12, 15, 94
oil extraction, 31, 56, 89, 91, 97
oil spills, 4–9, 12–15, 19
    effects on wildlife, 9, 11, 14
    financial costs of, 57
    map, 13

Paris Climate Agreement, 90, 92
    United States withdrawing from, 94
    US Climate Alliance, 97–98
partisan politics, 53, 66, 72, 80–81, 87, 90,
    96
pesticides, 17–18, 23, 33, 55, 71, 95
pesticides poisoning farmworkers, 27, 33, 93
pipelines, 14, 42, 50–51, 56–57, 89–90, 92
political engagement, 36, 53, 59, 103–105
polluted rivers, 33, 47
    Androscoggin River, 34
    Cuyahoga River, 8, 28, 48, 74
    Kalamazoo River, 57
pop culture environmentalism, 67, 70, 73
protests, 12, 15, 18, 20–21, 30, 36–39, 41–43,
    50, 61–62, 65–66, 76, 80, 96, 99, 104

racism in conservation groups, 85, 99
racism in pollution, 27, 40–42, 50, 61, 66,
    89, 93, 99
Reagan, Ronald, 88, 92
    climate change, 80–82
    decreasing regulation, 79–81
    Environmental Protection Agency and, 80

recycling, 36, 63–65, 67–70, 107
resource management, 84
reusing, 63, 107
river pollution, 8, 33–34, 42, 47, 48–49, 57, 74
rural communities, 75–76, 84, 88

Sagebrush Rebellion, 73, 75–76
sewage treatment plants, 37, 41, 55, 66
Sierra Club
  history, 85
  Aaron Mair, 85, 99
  racism, 85, 99
smog. *See* air quality
Standing Rock Sioux Reservation, 42
Styrofoam, 68

tar sands, 56–57, 89
teach-ins, 20–30, 38, 54
throwaway products, 16, 63, 107
trash, 16–17, 33, 43–44, 60, 63–65, 70, 103, 107

Trump, Donald, 42, 91–92, 94, 98

Union Oil, 4–7, 10–14
Union Square, 35–36

vehicle emissions. *See* emissions
vehicle manufacturing changes, 62–63
vehicle protests, 35–39
voting, 46, 64, 79, 103, 105, 107

waste management, 33, 55, 95
Waters of the United States, 88–89, 94
Woodsy Owl, 64

youth activists, 31, 42, 56–57, 69, 91, 105
Youth Climate Intervenors, 56–57
youth climate lawsuit, 91

ABOUT THE AUTHOR

Christy Peterson grew up with the environmental movement. Her father worked to restore salmon runs in the Yakima River basin in Washington State and fought to uphold and protect treaty rights for Northwest tribes. Her mother also helped shape Peterson's worldview through her commitment to social justice and her interest in nutrition and pesticide-free gardening.

Growing up, she was just as likely to find a biological specimen as a frozen dessert in the freezer, and she shared her home with rehabilitating and nesting birds and other creatures. This is probably why her backyard today is a certified habitat with the Washington State Department of Fish & Wildlife.

It's also probably why Peterson's work tends to focus on nature and ecology. In 2014 Peterson wrote "10 Things Kids Can Do to Help the Earth," an online publication from Kids Discover. Her book *24 Hours in a Salt Marsh* (2017) explores the salt marsh ecosystem, including the species it supports and its ecological benefits, both to the environment and to people.

Peterson also writes about other science and technology topics. Her books *Cutting-Edge Augmented Reality* and *Cutting-Edge Virtual Reality* were released in 2018. *Breakthroughs in Stars Research* and *Cutting-Edge Hubble Telescope Data* came out in 2019.

PHOTO ACKNOWLEDGMENTS

Image credits: Vernon Merritt III/The LIFE Picture Collection/Getty Images, p. 5; Laura Westlund/Independent Picture Service, pp. 6, 13, 33, 95; Bettmann Archive/Getty Images, p. 8; Vernon Merritt III/The LIFE Picture Collection/Getty Images, pp. 9, 10; Diane Cook and Len Jenshel/Getty Images, p. 16; Bettmann/Getty Images, p. 20; AP Photo/Bill Allen, p. 21; The Advertising Archives/Alamy Stock Photo, p. 23; SuperStock/Alamy Stock Photo, p. 24; Arthur Schatz/The LIFE Picture Collection/Getty Images, p. 27; Julian Wasser/The LIFE Images Collection/Getty Images, p. 28; Annie Wells/Los Angeles Times/Getty Images, p. 31; © Regents of the University of Michigan (Creative Commons Attribution 4.0 International License), p. 32; Archive Photos/Getty Images, p. 35; Duane Howell/The Denver Post/Getty Images, p. 38; GAROFALO Jack/Paris Match Archive/Getty Images, p. 40; Bettmann Archive/Getty Images, p. 41; Ricky Carioti/The Washington Post/Getty Images, p. 42; Julian Wasser/The LIFE Images Collection/Getty Images, p. 44; Ted Spiegel/CORBIS/Getty Images, p. 48; CORBIS/Getty Images, p. 51; Orjan F. Ellingvag/Corbis/Getty Images, p. 56; Joe Sohm/Visions of America/Universal Images Group/Getty Images, p. 57; Library of Congress, p. 63; U.S. National Archives and Records Administration/Wikimedia Commons (Public Domain), p. 66; Bill_Dally/iStock/Getty Images, p. 69; FRANKHILDEBRAND/Getty Images, p. 71; drnadig/iStock/Getty Images, p. 74; Harry Langdon/Getty Images, p. 79; The Print Collector/Getty Images, p. 85; SAUL LOEB/AFP/Getty Images, p. 90; Mark Wilson/Getty Images, p. 91; rightdx/Getty Images, p. 93; Sierra Club/Wikimedia Commons (CC Attribution), p. 99; Olin Feuerbacher/Getty Images, p. 100; Kristian Bell/Shutterstock.com, p. 101; Design: HAKKI ARSLAN/Shutterstock.com; adehoidar/Shutterstock.com; Bokeh Blur Background/Shutterstock.com.

Cover: HAKKI ARSLAN/Shutterstock.com; adehoidar/Shutterstock.com; Bokeh Blur Background/Shutterstock.com.